THE CHAOS* CURE

**Can't Have Anyone Over Syndrome*

THE CHAOS* CURE

CLEAN YOUR HOUSE AND CALM YOUR SOUL IN 15 MINUTES

Marla Cilley

aka *The FlyLady*

***Can't Have Anyone Over Syndrome**

Seal Press

Cover design by Alex Camlin.
Cover illustration © Alex Camlin.
Cover © 2018 Hachette Book Group, Inc.

Seal Press
Hachette Book Group
1290 Avenue of the Americas, New York, NY 10104
sealpress.com
@sealpress

Printed in the United States of America
First edition: December 2018

Published by Seal Press, an imprint of Perseus Books, LLC, a subsidiary of Hachette Book Group, Inc. The Seal Press name and logo is a trademark of the Hachette Book Group.

Editorial production by Christine Marra, *Marra*thon Production Services.
www.marrathoneditorial.org
Book design by Lisa Diercks, Endpaper Studio, www.endpaperstudio.com
Set in Filson Soft, Catalina Clemente, and Harman

ISBNs: 978-1-58005-802-5 (paperback), 978-1-58005-801-8 (ebook)
Library of Congress Control Number: 2018959608
LSC-C
10 9 8 7 6 5 4 3 2 1

This book is dedicated to my FlyBabies.

You deserve to have a home that blesses you!

We have the cure!

CONTENTS

THE CHAOS* CURE

**Can't Have Anyone Over Syndrome*

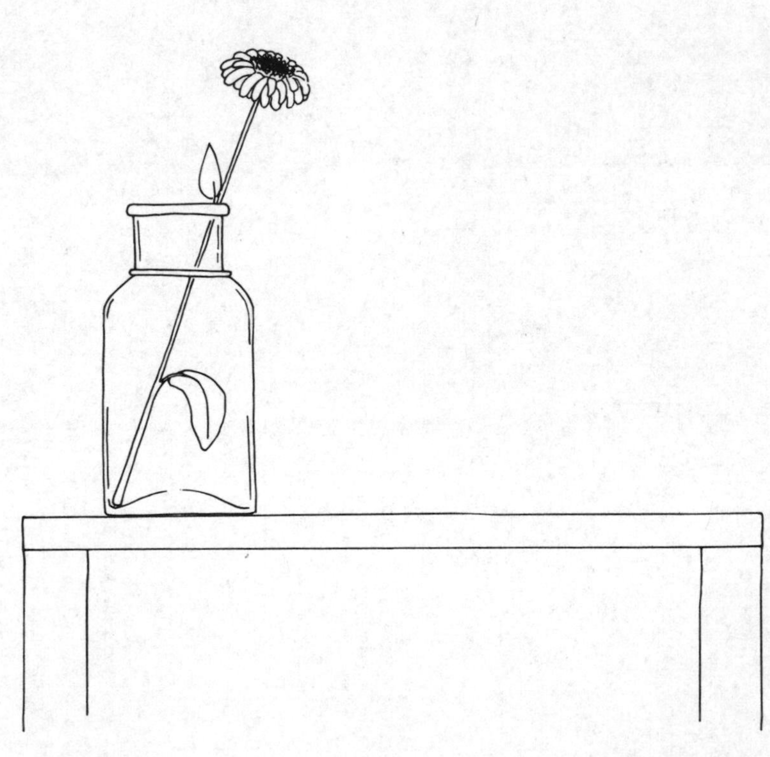

INTRODUCTION

FEEL YOUR WAY TO CLEAN AND CALM

I have a question for you: Did you grow up hating to clean?

I bet you said yes. Most of us did. Maybe our parents had a white glove standard. Maybe they said things like "do it right the first time or don't do it at all." When we were told to clean our rooms and our efforts fell short of perfect, maybe we were punished, or maybe we were forced into all-day cleaning marathons until every item in our rooms was perfectly placed, with hospital corners on the sheets and socks folded *just so*.

Then there was "cleaning day." Most of our parents, and their parents, chose one day a week to take on the major tasks of housekeeping. No, let me correct this. . . . They chose one day a week to shout out orders while *we* did the cleaning. The kind words were few and far between as we hustled around trying to please our masters by shining the windows, mopping the floors, polishing the silver, dusting the bookshelves, and so on. A whole day was devoted to household labors.

Even now, I cringe as I think about it.

Let me ask you another question: What was the result of being forced with an iron hand to clean?

For most of us, the answer is easy: We don't ever want to clean again. Can you blame us for feeling bad about the entire undertaking?

But now, as adults, we still are challenged by keeping a nice home. We look around our homes and see clutter and CHAOS (Can't Have Anyone Over Syndrome) everywhere, and we're no better off. There's a heavy burden that comes with a messy home—maybe we spare ourselves the effort of wiping and scrubbing and decluttering, but instead we're surrounded by distractions and dirt, not to mention the feelings that come with a messy home, like

Shame when friends drop by and we have to quickly stash the junk that's piled on the sofa to find a place for our friends to sit

Guilt when we see dirt and clutter and know we should take care of it but we don't

Resentment that housecleaning is time-consuming and we have other obligations that dominate our attention

Jealousy of others who have sparkling homes, full of Pinterest-perfect rooms and organized closets and cabinets

Discouragement that we'll never be able to conquer all that CHAOS

This is how we see our predicament. We can't not clean, and we don't want to feel angry or resentful when we do. So, it is time for us to make a change. We have to release the all-or-nothing thinking we learned from our parents and put aside our negative, paralyzing feelings that prevent us from making progress. In their place, we have to find a new way to function, a new way that shows respect for our hectic schedules and full lives.

My goal is to give you a new way to get your home looking nice—so nice that you would not be embarrassed to have someone drop by unexpectedly—all in 15 minutes or less. But that's not all. I also want you to embrace the effort, enjoying the fun of getting things done in your home.

Now, you may not believe me that this is possible. But I know it is.

You deserve to live in a home that honors you, and I will teach you how to recognize the gifts of your home. I will help you discover the joy of maintaining your house in a way that makes *you* happy. I will guide you to establish simple habits that will set up your home to be ready for company—without having to shout orders or play the martyr. When those habits are strung into simple routines, your home will practically clean itself. I'm not kidding!

You can do this. We will make it happen together. I am so proud of you.

Love,

The FlyLady

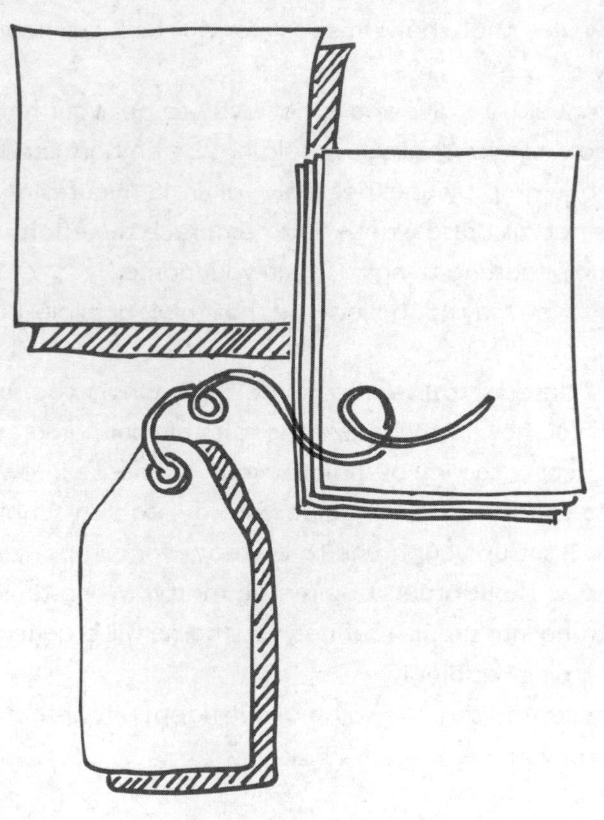

WHAT YOU'LL FIND IN THIS BOOK

THE GENIUS OF STICKY NOTES AND OTHER SIMPLE SYSTEMS

Being organized is a dream for all of us. We love the mental image of an orderly home, but we don't know how to get our acts together and keep our homes shipshape. Sometimes we give up before we ever get started because we have no confidence in ourselves.

Don't do that. Don't give up! I'll tell you the secret to keeping your home in order (and it's not much of a secret because we all know it!): Establish better habits.

A habit is something you do without thinking about it, and that's what you need to keep your house picked up and clean. The hard part is making the habits stick. If changing our habits were easy, we'd all exercise daily, drink plenty of water, put down our cell phones for long stretches of time, and live our best lives without even trying. Can you imagine how nice that would be?

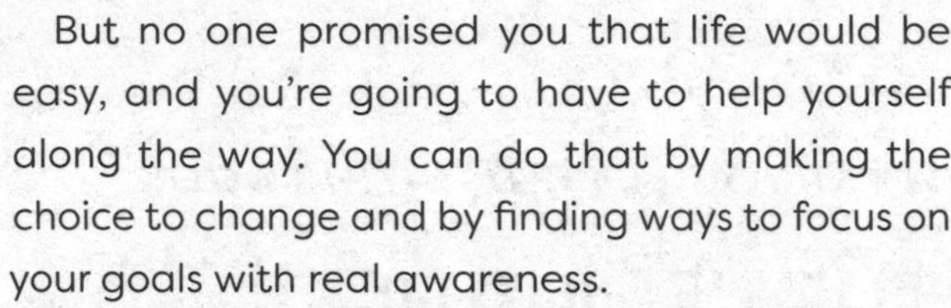

But no one promised you that life would be easy, and you're going to have to help yourself along the way. You can do that by making the choice to change and by finding ways to focus on your goals with real awareness.

You need a focused effort to practice a new habit if you want to make the change stick.

Let me tell you a story. Several decades ago, I needed to practice the new law of buckling my seat belt. I would catch myself backing out of the driveway without having fastened mine or my son's, and I was determined to make this habit stick. It was for our safety and well-being, and I was committed to the change. So here's what I did: I taped a brightly colored piece of paper to the dashboard in my car and wrote the words SEAT BELTS on the paper. That's it!

This note gave me a directive, and I followed it. Every time I got in the car, the little piece of paper reminded me to fasten my seat belt and check my son's. Pretty soon, the habit was established, and I didn't need the paper anymore because the practice had stuck. I was buckling up without even noticing I was doing it.

What a difference! What a gift!

I started trying this technique in other areas of my life. When I wanted to get in the habit of shining my sink every day so it would look brand new, I put a small, colorful reminder on the kitchen window above the sink—a little note that said "Shine your sink!" I added a smiley face. That was the feeling I got when I walked into the kitchen when the sink was shining. After a few days, the note went away, but my shiny sink was permanent—and it still makes me smile.

How could something so simple and unimportant as a little note stuck on a window make such a difference in my life?

1. I didn't have to rely on my memory right away.

2. I did not pile on more than was humanly possible to do.

3. I practiced it every day.

4. I had inadvertently given myself a reward. I had *hope* and a smile on my face.

That one insignificant little piece of paper transformed my home and my life. I kept using this note system, putting sticky notes around my house with little friendly reminders that kept me on task and moving toward establishing good patterns and routines.

This technique can help you, too. Throughout this book, you'll see ***Stick with It!*** suggestions for messages you can put on little pieces of paper or sticky notes to help you establish new patterns and habits in your home. When you see these prompts, give them a try. Grab a note, scribble the message I've offered as a reminder or write your own, and put it where you can see it at a glance.

It won't stay there forever—just as long as it takes for the action to become automatic. For some things, it'll take just a day or two, while other habits might take longer to settle in.

It doesn't matter what you use for your notes. Grab a plain old yellow office sticky or buy some at a drugstore in funky sizes or shaped like cats or in neon colors—whatever makes you smile. The real beauty of the sticky-note system is that it's easy, cheap, and effective. No complicated systems, no expensive materials, just plain old common sense.

Stick with it!

CLEAN IN 15: USE YOUR TIMER

You'll also find in the pages of this book a picture of a timer that looks like the one here.

When you see this timer, you'll be reminded that there's no need to spend more than 15 minutes on your task. Too often we avoid projects because they seem too overwhelming or too time-consuming. Enough of that. Most jobs can be done in less than 15 minutes. Just 15! If it's taking you longer than 15 minutes, you might be doing something wrong. So set your timer and you'll be amazed at how much progress you make before the bell goes off.

On the Fly!

There are all kinds of ways we can make our housekeeping jobs easier. Some people call them hacks or tips or tricks. I call them smart. I've collected all kinds of shortcuts and clever techniques to help you get your home looking the way you want it to, and you'll find them in the *On the Fly!* tips throughout this book.

Got Kids? *Kids need to learn how to clean. And we need their help to keep our houses in order. Start training them when they are small and encourage them to have fun. In this book you'll find lots of ways to involve kids in the cleaning process—ways that will bring out the sparkle in your home while making the kinds of family memories you'll all treasure.*

DON'T GET DAUNTED, GET DRESSED

To feel in control of your home, you need to feel strong and capable and ready to do the jobs that need doing. For every task, the first step is this: **Get dressed.**

This may not seem important, but it's the foundation for feeling good about yourself. Staying in your robe all day—even if you aren't leaving the house—makes you feel like a slug. Getting up and getting dressed makes you feel whole. That means getting dressed to your shoes: Walking around in your sock feet may be comfy, but it won't give you the can-do energy you need to face your day and your home and your life with confidence and strength.

Trust me on this. Your whole day will be more productive if you will just do this little thing. As soon as you get up in the morning, get dressed to the shoes.

On the Fly!

If for some reason you don't wear shoes in your home, whether for religious or cultural reasons, get a pair of plain sneakers that you wear only in the house. When you get home, put them on. Mr. Rogers did it, and you can, too! If you don't want to spend the money on a new pair of lace-up shoes, then wash a pair that you will use only in the house.

PERFECTIONISM IS LIKE QUICKSAND

Impossible Standards for You and Your Home

Do you love home makeover shows on TV and before-and-after remodeling stories in magazines? Depending on your attitude, either they can be fun and inspiring or they can make you feel terrible about your home and powerless to change it. We look at the pictures and it seems impossible to attain a room that evokes the calm that the rooms in those images do. But when we let go of our perfectionism, we can take baby steps to transform our home. Please don't throw in the towel because you don't know where to start.

First, let's look at some of these "after" photos. There are no jackets on the hooks, no kids' toys except in clearly labeled canvas bins, and no books except stylish artist retrospectives. The dining table is glamorously set for a party of 12, but there's no food in evidence other than a giant bowl of green apples that may or may not be real. With this glossy, finished setup, these spaces are designed to be photographed, not lived in. Don't allow perfect lighting and a fleet of professional home stylists blind you to the fact that your home can be beautiful, too.

On the other hand, all of these "after" photos share a common theme, and that's clean surfaces and a lack of clutter.

The easiest, most affordable way to beautify your home is to eliminate the clutter. Try it in your kitchen and you'll see the difference right away. Set your timer for 10 minutes, put on some motivating music, and go to it.

1. Take all the magnets, photos, and takeout menus off your refrigerator. See how much better it looks already?

2. Starting at one end of your kitchen, put away everything on your counters. Only leave the appliances that you use more than twice a week.

3. Place all your canisters in a neat row.

4. Wipe down your counters.

5. Clear off the windowsills.

6. Wipe down your stove.

7. Use a glass cleaner and paper towels on the inside of your kitchen windows.

8. Finish by shining your sink (see page 75).

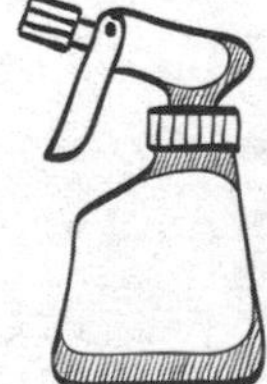

Stand back and admire your kitchen's refreshing new look. Do a similar spiffing routine in a different room each day, and you'll soon have the calming home makeover you crave.

On the Fly!

Don't let yourself get immune to clutter on your kitchen counters. Sweep it aside and clear it out regularly to keep your kitchen a happy place to be.

Stick with it!
Where to put it:
On any cluttered spot
What to write:
Decluttering is cheaper than remodeling

THE ART OF HAPPY HOUSEGUESTING

You get a call from a favorite cousin who is coming to town in a couple of weeks, and you joyfully extend an invitation to your house. This is going to be so much fun! Your excitement makes you giggle like when you were little. Then you hang up, look around, and reality sets in.

What have I done?

I can hear your thoughts from where I'm sitting:

- *The basement needs repainting.*
- *The towels are not good enough.*
- *I need new sheets.*
- *There's no convenient bathroom for my guests to use.*
- *I have no idea what to feed them.*

Put a stop to the panic. Everything is going to be just fine. Sit down with a cup of something warm and take a few minutes to gather your thoughts. Preparing your home for guests needn't be a huge ordeal. Remember that they are coming to see you, not to judge you on every little detail.

Your first job is to let go of your perfectionism.

Then, start with the excess. Over the next few days, gradually get rid of the clutter that makes your home look messy. Check your Hot Spots (see page 62)—are they cluttered or clear? Do a walk-through of your house, picking up trash and loose dishes, like that mug that lives on your nightstand and the extra cup in the bathroom. Dump the trash, wash the dishes, put them away. Easy.

Now that the air is clear and the space more open, give your surfaces a quick wipe. Go room by room and see how they change and take on a new, clean shape with just a simple swipe with a damp cloth.

Your house is looking good! Now you can keep it clean by paying attention to each room as you enter it. When you're in the bathroom, give the commode a Swish and Swipe (see page 41). When you're in the kitchen, pour the cereal from its ugly box into a big mason jar (see page 83). Just by paying attention and reaching out to address what needs improving, you'll have your house cozy and calm and ready for welcoming guests.

Once they arrive, enjoy your visit. Relax, welcome your visitors, and let the rest go! Above all else: *Do not keep apologizing for your home.* It's a representation of you and the things you care about. If your home is clean, then you've succeeded at putting your best foot forward.

You may be surprised by how much you enjoy the way your home feels when it's guest-ready. Keep this great feeling in mind after your guests leave and continue to implement these simple techniques. You really can live every day like a guest in your own home.

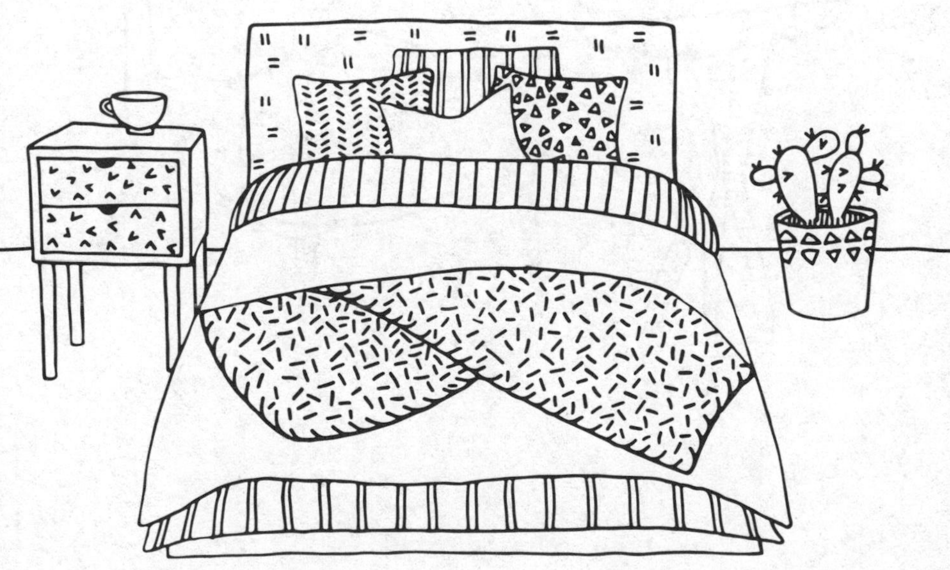

HOME

THE FLYLADY'S PANIC-FREE PHILOSOPHY

There should be a rule against friends dropping by for surprise visits. You know how this goes. "I'm in your neighborhood, okay if I swing over?"

"Sure! Great! See you soon!"

Isn't that nice?

It is! And frustrating and embarrassing and scary if your home is a mess.

Because there isn't a rule, we have to master the art of **Crisis Cleaning.** This is a method of speed cleaning that boosts the appearance of your home—and your dignity—before the doorbell rings.

When you find out an unexpected guest is headed your way, you'll be tempted to do a Stash and Dash—that's when you run around the house grabbing all the odds and ends that are cluttering our home, the dirty clothes, the piles of paper, and shove them in your shower stalls or under your couches. Don't do it! There's a better way.

Get ready to crisis clean the FlyLady way. The first rule is to stay focused: You cannot let your perfectionism take over, and you cannot be distracted by every mess you pass. This is strategic surface clearing, not the time to scrub hard, dig deep, or clean out a closet. And for the love of Pete, don't redecorate!

If you have 5 minutes: Focus on the room where your guest is going to spend most of his or her time—this is usually the living room or the kitchen. Grab an empty laundry basket and head straight there. Clear off all of the tables and surfaces, loading up the laundry basket as you go. If you're in the living room, fluff the pillows and fold the throw blanket on your couch. Put the laundry basket in your bedroom and close the door.

If you have 10 minutes: Go to the bathroom and make it presentable by wiping the counters and putting your grooming tools in a cabinet or that laundry basket that's sitting in your bedroom. Take dirty clothes to the laundry room and do a quick Swish and Swipe in the commode. (Don't be fussy about products—a squirt of shampoo will do!)

If you have 15 minutes: Head to the kitchen and load the dishwasher. If it's already full of clean dishes, leave them there and fill the sink with hot soapy water to camouflage the dirty plates—it's always nicer to look at bubbly water doing its job. Wipe down the counters and put on the tea kettle for something soothing to drink.

If you're lucky enough to have time left over: Take care of you! Take a breath, freshen up, and sit down with a cup of tea. You will be calm, cool, and clutter-free when your guest shows up.

MAKE A PLAN FOR POSITIVE PROGRESS

Let me ask you this question: Are you constantly running around putting out fires? Do you regularly . . .

- → Search for lost keys
- → Apologize for missed appointments
- → Run out of toilet paper
- → Forget to buy printer ink
- → Arrive late for work or other appointments
- → Forget friends' and family birthdays
- → Lose a credit card
- → Misplace your wallet
- → Run out of gas
- → Forget to take vitamins and medications

If you answered yes to any of the above, I'm going to guess that you don't have household routines.

Routines are not prisons from which you try to escape. Routines are the framework for a peaceful life. Routines establish a series of habits that are strung into a logical succession of actions. When we don't establish routines, we inevitably make mistakes.

Bear with me while I tell you a little story about my two left feet. In college, I took an aerobics class, but I could not kick and clap my hands at the same time. I would step left when I should have been stepping right. I wanted to drop the class because I felt so awkward.

One day after class the sweet, ballerina-like instructor pulled me aside and helped me learn this lesson. She explained that I was trying to learn everything at one time and that I needed to break the dance down into sections. Learn one section, then practice another section until it was automatic. After that, add the sections together. Eventually, I learned the whole dance. I was named the most improved student, which was quite an honor for me because I was the oldest and most out of shape of all the people in that 8 a.m. class! (The fact that I was able to get to a class at eight in the morning was another moment of pride for me.)

Every lesson we learn comes when we are ready for it. Who said, "When the student is ready the teacher will come"? That day, I wrapped my head around a concept that changed my life forever: Take on the task part by part, repeating each one until the habit becomes second nature.

A couple of years after I learned the dance routine, I applied this lesson to my quest to get my act together. I was so tired of living in chaos. On New Year's Day I made my proverbial resolution to Get Organized. That fateful day, I examined why I was so disorganized, and the conclusion I came to was that I had never established any habits. Putting out fires was how I lived—I reacted to needs rather than planned for them.

It was as though I was skipping my vitamins and getting sick. Sure, I could take medicine later, but I could have avoided the fever if I'd been in the habit of taking my vitamins. Even if I wasn't physically sick, my stress level was high, and I was exhausted from my constant internal battle of negative thinking and shame from the mistakes I'd made. I was ready for something different.

My solution was to practice one habit a month.

Psychologists tell us that it takes 21 days to establish a new habit. They must not have been perfectionists like us. With our all-or-nothing thinking, when we miss a day, we just give up. If we can't do it perfectly, why bother? That way of living sets us up for continual failure.

A whole month incorporated a generous grace period. Missing one day was no reason to throw in the towel—I could forgive and forget and return to my daily commitment to the task. Each month I picked a new habit—just one. It took me almost a year of being gracious with myself to string my habits into routines, but I did it.

- → January—Shine the kitchen sink
- → February—Declutter
- → March—Get dressed to the shoes
- → April—Make the bed
- → May—Move my body
- → June—Drink water
- → July—Swish and swipe bathroom surfaces
- → August—Do a load of laundry each day
- → September—Practice a before-bed routine
- → October—Clear paper clutter
- → November—Plan menus
- → December—Pamper myself

I committed to one task for 30 days at a time. Boy, it sure worked! Now I do all of this *without even noticing I'm doing it.*

Routines help us get things done without having to think about what to do next. We are on automatic pilot. This is such a fun way to live. Our homes become the peaceful environment that we have dreamed about. We can have friends over without two days of cleaning up. We can be spontaneous for the first time in our lives!

That's the beauty of routines—we make habits out of the everyday maintenance of our lives so we can stop *thinking* about them and let our minds focus more actively on fun, excitement, and pleasure. If you didn't have to remember to buy toilet paper and send birthday cards, think of the brainpower you'd free up to focus on more exciting things.

As routines are incorporated into your home life, the CHAOS and stress will subside. This order comes from being on automatic pilot. We don't have to think about what to do next; we just do it. This becomes a beautiful dance to your day. The cleaner your home becomes, the calmer your life will be.

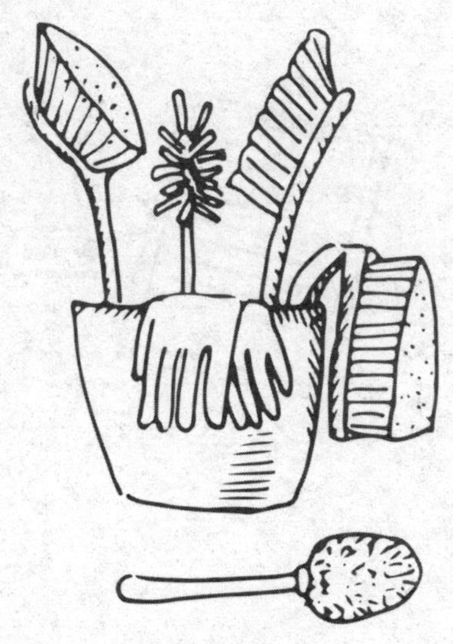

FEEL THE STRETCH

Cleaning Is Good for the Home, Body, and Soul

A few years ago, I got my first fitness tracker. I was blown away by how few steps I was taking each day. This got me thinking about different ways that I could increase my steps. Because I work from home and hate to go to the gym, I decided to experiment with ways to increase my steps and get my body moving.

Along with getting my steps, I needed to stretch, build muscle, and get in some aerobic activity. I soon discovered that cleaning was the perfect way to get it all done.

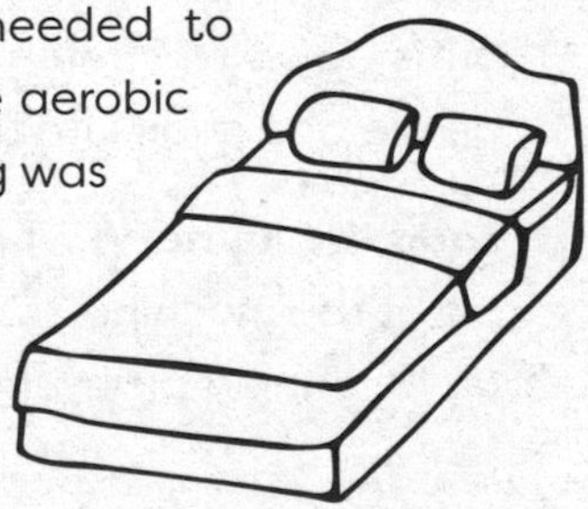

Make the bed: After sleeping all night, we need to stretch our bodies.

Have you ever watched cats or dogs when they wake up? They stretch! I use my stretching to make the bed while I am still in it. Think of it as horizontal jumping jacks or making snow angels under your covers. Smooth out the covers with your legs and arms, then hold the covers up to your chin and slide out the side. Take a few minutes to fluff or punch your pillows (it's the softer side of boxing!). If you have decorative pillows to put on the bed, hold them with both hands and raise them over your head to stretch. Then bend down and touch your toes and hold this stretch for a count of 10.

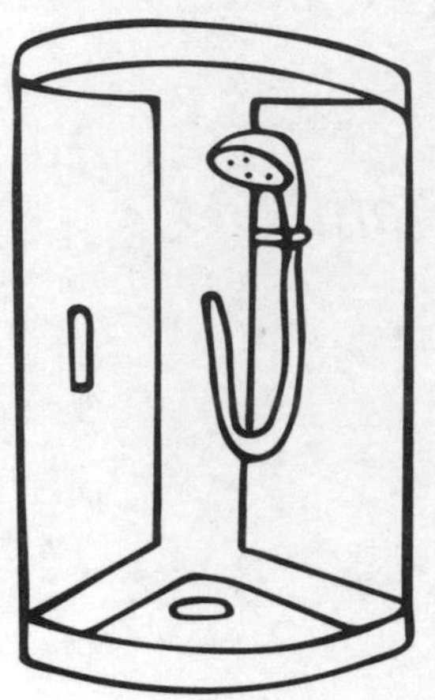

Clean the shower (and yourself): Take a hot shower to warm up your muscles, and let's get your arms moving. Grab a FlyLady Purple Microfiber Rag (see page 37, "Arm Yourself: FlyLady's Top Five Must-Haves") or a soap scrunchy (a nylon mesh ball with soap inside) to scrub an area of your shower walls. Use both arms. Stretch high and low. (No dancing in the shower though—that's not safe!) Bend over and drop your arms down to stretch your spine. Be gentle and relax into the stretch.

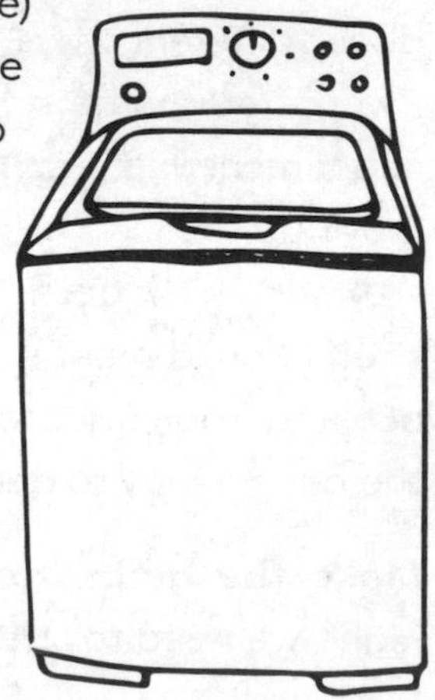

Load the laundry: While you're standing at the machine, take a moment to do 10 leaning push-ups.

Lift the laundry: My washer and dryer are in the basement, and I use the stairs as a Stair-master by walking up and down them. Use the laundry basket as a weight-lifting tool, raising it from your waist to shoulder height and down again—but don't do this while walking up and down the stairs. When you walk up and down the stairs, focus on what you are doing and hold the hand rail.

Walk the dog: We have a new puppy that needs a good brisk walk first thing in the morning, which is a great way to get my day off to an energetic start. Sometimes I take a rag with me and use it to clean the front porch on our way back in. I stretch high to reach the top of the door jamb, and stretch again to clean away cobwebs from hanging lights.

Get gardening: Make it a point to stay mindful of your body and stretch wherever you can as you deadhead flowers, pull weeds, and harvest ripe fruits and vegetables. This also gets you outside into the fresh air and sunshine. Taking time to (literally!) smell the roses is good for your body and soul.

Empty the dishwasher: More opportunities to bend and stretch. Reach high to put dishes away and bend low to store pots and pans. You can add a few deep knee bends as you reach into the dishwasher for each item.

Mop while the coffee is brewing: Grab your mop; you can use it either wet or dry. While the coffeemaker is burbling away, run around your house as fast as you can mopping the floor. This is not your mother's floor mopping! Let go of your perfectionism.

Dance away the dust: Grab your feather duster and give everything a once-over as you run or dance around the house. Then take the duster outside and alternate arms as you shake, shake, shake off that dust.

Micro moves: Have you ever just stood at the microwave watching your food go around in circles? Take advantage of this time to buff up your body as well as your house. Use the edge of the counter to do leg lifts, leaning push-ups, or squats. Sweep the kitchen, wipe down counters, or run around clearing out the cobwebs.

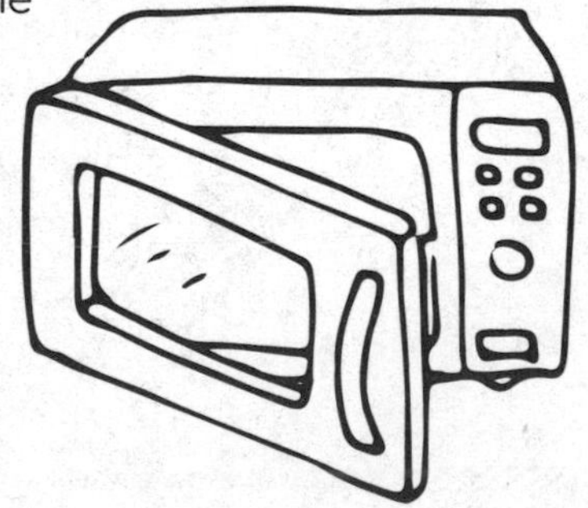

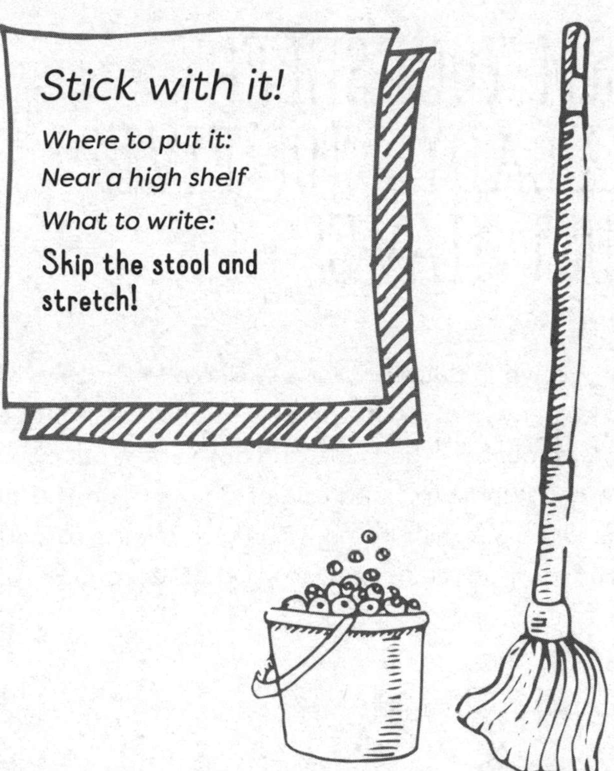
Stick with it!
Where to put it:
Near a high shelf
What to write:
Skip the stool and stretch!

ARM YOURSELF! FLYLADY'S TOP FIVE MUST-HAVES

You can get your cleaning done a whole lot faster and easier and better when you're using the right tools for each job. Don't strain your bank account, and don't stress out about how to choose among the hundreds of products on the grocery shelves. Just stock your home with these five items and you'll always have what you need. Doesn't that feel good?

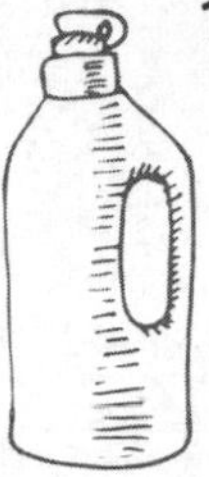

1. DISHWASHING LIQUID

I use it to fight stains, wash dishes, and clean the toilet when I run out of old shampoo.

2. WINDOW CLEANER *OR* A MIXTURE OF VINEGAR AND WATER

Sometimes we need something to spray to make ourselves feel like we are doing something.

3. FLYLADY'S OSTRICH FEATHER DUSTER

Ostrich feathers collect dust and don't stir it up. Two minutes with your Ostrich Feather Duster and the dreaded dusting becomes a happy dance. Then take your duster outside and bless the world.

4. FLYLADY'S RUBBA SCRUBBA

There is always something that needs a good rub. Grab one of these rubber brushes to clean your veggies, another to de-cat-fur your furniture, and a third to scrub your knees and elbows.

5. FLYLADY'S PURPLE MICROFIBER RAGS

Who needs paper towels for those dirtiest jobs? These rags make cleaning windows a breeze—with or without glass spray. Plain water does not streak when you use a handy purple rag!

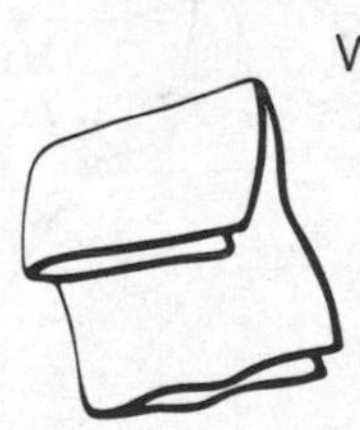

BATHROOM SURFACE SPRUCE

Truth time: If your mother asked to use your bathroom, would you want to lock the door and send her to the nearest diner instead?

The good news is that once you know how to go about it, it doesn't take a lot of effort to keep your bathroom clean and beautiful. And whether or not Mom makes an appearance, you deserve a space that honors you, your health, and your happiness. Start by getting rid of the clutter to make it easy to maintain the new order with a simple daily Swish and Swipe.

On the Fly!

If you use hairspray, your floor gets sticky. Place your bath towel on the floor before you spray, or step into the shower and close the shower curtain.

Stick with it!
Where to put it:
By the toilet
What to write:
Swish and Swipe

Here's what you're going to do:

1. Set your timer for 10 minutes.

2. Begin by clearing off all the items on the counters, finding each a permanent home in a drawer or cabinet. If there's a shortage of storage space, quickly clear out any old expired items taking up precious real estate. (That 12-year-old mousse you've been thinking you "might use someday"? That can go.)

3. Wipe the dust off the counters and the toothpaste splatters from the sink.

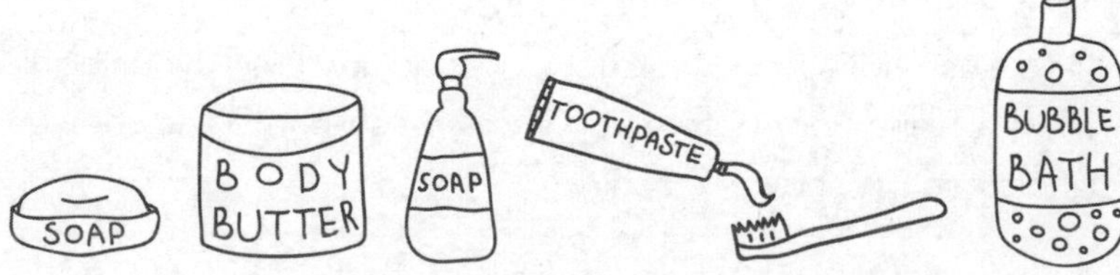

4. Swish your toilet bowl with some shampoo and a toilet brush, and wipe down the seat.

5. Do a quick sweep of the floor. If it takes you longer than 60 seconds, you're being a perfectionist. (Stop it!)

6. If there's time still left on the clock, take an old wet towel with a little shampoo on it and use it to mop the floor with your feet. (Yes, you can use shampoo. Soap is soap!) Then, toss the dirty towel in the washer.

7. Stand back and admire your clean, fresh-smelling bathroom.

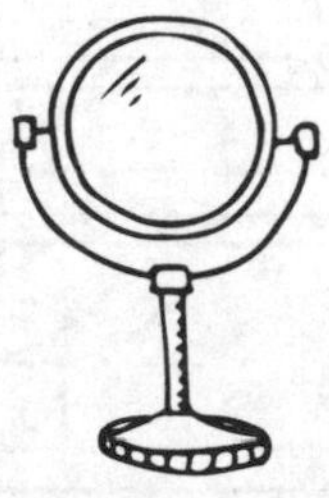

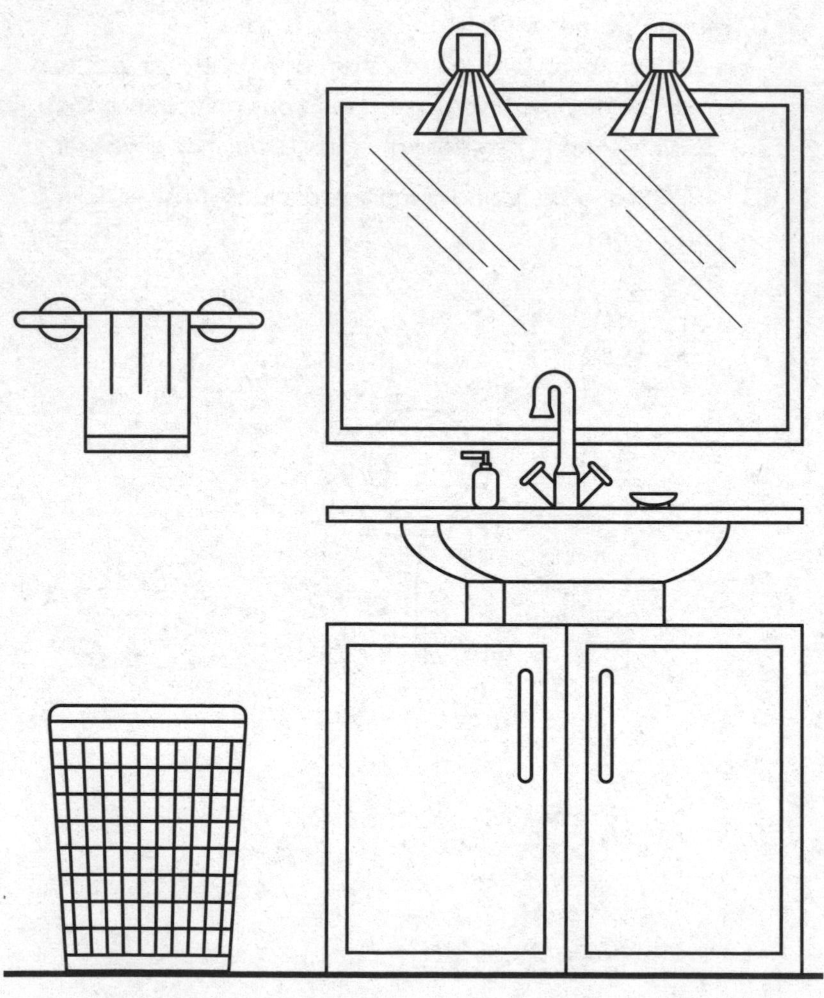

BATHROOM SUPER SCRUB

Today we're headed into our bathrooms for a good scrub. Set your timer for 15 minutes and here we go.

First, make sure you have your tools handy. I recommend keeping these in the bathroom so they're always readily available—you can't do this if you have young children or pets that might get into them, but if there are no kids around, you'll see how easy the job is when the tools are where they belong. You can also keep window cleaner and paper towels under the sink for quick wipes of the counter, mirrors, and floor.

SUPPLIES

1. Window cleaner
2. Toilet bowl brush
3. Toilet bowl brush holder (old vase or utensil holder)

4. Paper towels, washcloths, or cleaning wipes

5. Soap is soap (fill an old vase with a 50-50 solution of old shampoo, body wash, or bubble bath and water)

6. Mesh shower ball

TACKLE THE TOILET

All it takes is a swish, swipe, and flush to get your toilet clean and ready for company (you count as company, too). If you can't do this in less than 2 minutes, you're making it harder than it has to be. To clean my toilet, I like to use up those old bottles of shampoo, body wash, and bubble bath that have been hiding under the bathroom sink. I declutter those bottles by emptying them into my vase. Then I add the same amount of water to the vase. This is where I store my toilet bowl brush. To swish my toilet, all I do is hold up the toilet bowl brush to allow the excess to drip off and then swish the toilet.

In fact, it's such a quick job that I like to do it every morning and skip the monthly scrub. If you start with a clean bowl and then do it daily while you're getting dressed, you don't even need cleaner, so it goes even faster.

SPRUCE THE SINK

Here's another fast-swipe job. All you do is wipe out your sink with a spritz of window cleaner. I keep a stack of white washcloths next to the sink for drying my hands. Not only does using one washcloth per hand washing keep germs from spreading, but you can also use the cloth to wipe the sink dry. Once you get into this habit, you'll shine up the sink every time you use the bathroom.

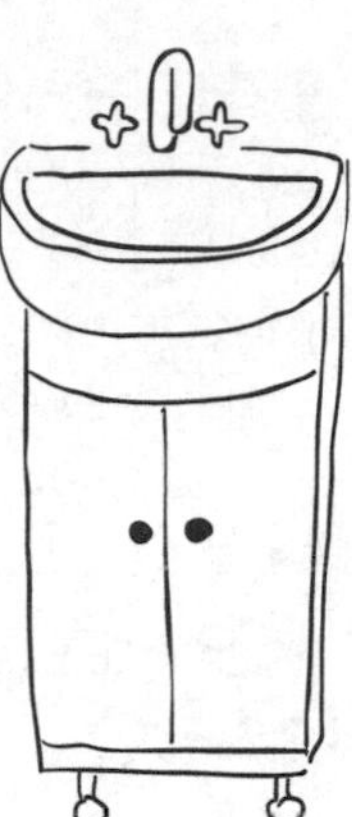

BABY THE BATHTUB

Does your tub gross you out? Get ready to tackle it as a big job for the last time. If you follow these instructions, cleaning the tub will be fast and easy from now on.

1. Start with any leftover shampoo, body wash, or bubble bath.

2. The time to clean your tub is when you're taking a bath or shower. This saves your back from the hard work of scrubbing from the side. Plus, it saves water.

3. If your shower has lots of soap film on the doors, it's already prepped for a quick scrub. Otherwise, pick one small area to wash every day while conditioning your hair. One minute a day with a mesh ball soon gets your shower clean and keeps it that way.

We are just so gullible when it comes to cleaning products. Our under-the-sink cabinets are filled with miracles-in-a-bottle, all guaranteed to make one small section of the house—counters, floors, windows, toilets—shine like the sun. Marketing experts want you to believe

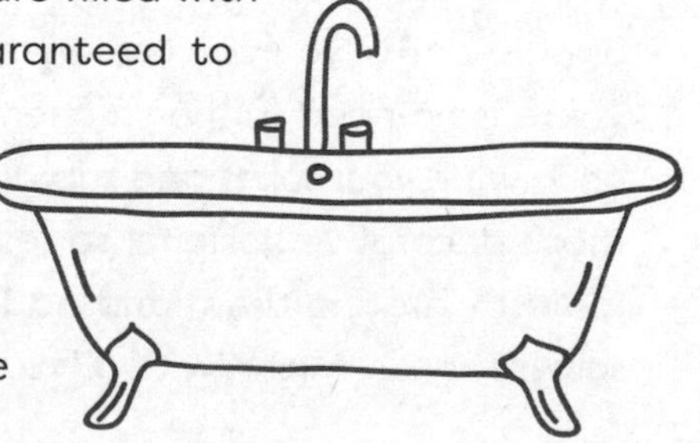

that the secret to a clean house is having the perfect potion for each individual task. In fact, I've learned that the opposite is true: Soap is soap. The less variety you have of it, the simpler your cleaning routine (and thus the cleaner your home) will be.

When I was in the first grade, my teacher, Mrs. Wyatt, made hand soap for us by grating half-used bars of soap into hot water to melt. She would squeeze a small amount of the solution into our little hands so we could wash before lunch. Folks, this is about as complicated as your cleaning products need to be.

As you declutter your bathrooms, you're going to find lots of unused soapy products: shampoos, body washes, bubble baths, and hand soaps. Maybe they didn't live up to the hype in the commercials, or maybe they were gifts you didn't really want in the first place. Meet your new all-purpose cleaners, about to go from using precious storage space to serving an important purpose. Use them to wipe the shower walls and the sides of the tub. A little dab on a washcloth will get rid of that bathtub ring. Dilute it by half with water, pour it in the container that holds your toilet bowl brush, and then just swish your toilet with it daily. I've even added unwanted conditioner to this mixture because it smells good.

When you finally run out of old shampoos, body washes, and bubble baths, you can use an inexpensive dishwashing liquid. There is no need for harsh chemical cleaners when you swish and swipe your toilet and tub daily. You can even make use of those decorative designer soaps that gather dust in the bathroom by grating them and adding them to hot water to dissolve. Thanks, Mrs. Wyatt! (FlyLady's first-grade teacher.)

Soap is soap! It's not precious. It lifts and releases dirt, one way or another.

On the Fly!

HERE ARE BONUS USES FOR SOAPS:

→ **Toothpaste**—great for getting rid of water circles on furniture, cleaning jewelry, and filling nail holes in walls.

→ **Dishwasher pods**—useful for removing burnt-on food stuck to casserole dishes. Once a month I also put two in my whirlpool tub after I get out and run it for an hour to clean the jets.

→ **Dishwashing liquid**—excellent for pretreating grease spots on clothing.

→ **Window cleaner**—easily removes spots (and puppy piddles) on floors.

HOUSEBREAK THE BEDROOM

The bedroom takes a lot of hits. It's one of the last places most of us clean because it's not a space for visitors, and it's a natural spot for stockpiling stray clothes. When company comes, we stash-and-dash the excess piles from the rest of the house into the bedroom and lock the door behind us.

Reinvent this room as your own private sanctuary, a peaceful place where order rules. After completing this routine just once, you'll be inspired to maintain a space that fires you up each morning and lets you rest easy each night.

Set your timer for 15 minutes, and let's get this place tidied up. We'll break this up into three phases:

- **Make the bed:** 3 minutes
- **Clear the surfaces:** 5 minutes
- **Declutter piles:** 7 minutes

MAKE THE BED

3 MINUTES

The answer is yes, you do have to make your bed every day. But what you may have forgotten is that making your bed only takes a few seconds, and changing your sheets, just a few minutes more. If you spend more than 3 minutes on the whole affair, you're doing it wrong. No one expects hospital corners! Just pull up the sheets and blankets, give them a nice, strong tug so they lay flat, fluff your pillows, and be on your way. See how fast that was?

I make my bed as soon as I get up in the morning, even before I head to the bathroom or get dressed. The bed is the centerpiece of the room, and even if the rest of the place is a mess, seeing a made bed makes me feel inspired and ready for the day.

CLEAR THE SURFACES

5 MINUTES

Dresser

If the last time you saw the top of your dresser was the day you first moved in, get ready to celebrate. Toss the trash, put away clothes, and shelve the books. Now doesn't that feel better? When you catch yourself placing something on the top of your dresser, stop and find it a real home. It only takes a few seconds to put it away someplace where you'll be able to find it quickly and easily.

Nightstand

If your cat can't swish her tail without hitting the books, magazines, and other odds and ends by your bed, it's time to pare down. Toss the trash, and move everything else to where it belongs until the only things left are what you need as you fall asleep: books, glasses, and a small candle if you'd like to have one. I like to keep water by the bed, too. (I prefer a bottle to a glass so it doesn't go *kersplash* during the night.)

DECLUTTER PILES

7 MINUTES

Purge the floor and furniture of clothing, magazines, towels, and other stuff that's made itself at home while you weren't looking. Throw away the trash and recycle the magazines. Shelve the books or place them by the front door to return to the library.

You can do this! Be tough. If you work for 7 minutes and you haven't finished, no problem. Tomorrow is a new day, and immediate perfection is not the goal. Make progress and pat yourself on the back when you see surfaces emerge.

Now that your room is clean and clear, you can rest more fully when you're in it. To keep it this way, just make your bed each morning and resist the temptation to "temporarily" place odds and ends where they don't belong.

Got Kids? *Even if your kids are as young as three or four, you can start teaching them how to make their beds. Show them how to make snow angels under the covers to smooth out the bedding, slide out the side, and tuck in the sheets. Then, have them fluff the pillow, and congratulate them on making a tidy (albeit perfectly imperfect!) bed.*

PILLOWS 101

Watch any remodel show on television and you'll notice the hosts are crazy about pillows. They put pillows on the sofa, in chairs, on beds . . . so many pillows on the beds! How many heads do they plan to put in those beds? All the extra pillows get in the way. And where do you put them when you go to bed? On the floor? What's the point? If pillows make you happy, then by all means stock up, but keep in mind the adage that less is more.

PILLOWS FOR SLEEP

But we do need *some* pillows to cradle our heads at night. There is no telling how much money I have spent on pillows over the years. I have tried feather pillows, chopped-foam pillows, memory foam pillows, wedge pillows, buckwheat pillows, and microbead pillows. I have used lumbar pillows, donut pillows, body pillows, neck pillows, travel pillows, and pillows with arms. I finally learned that fighting a pillow all night robs me of sleep. When a pillow helps me to fall asleep quickly and rest well, it is a keeper.

My bed has two sleeping pillows, two big pillows with decorative shams that match a bedspread quilt, and one little pillow with a cute saying on it: "I'm Not Bossy, I Just Have Better Ideas!" My friend gave me that needlepoint pillow. It makes me laugh every time I place it on the bed. My granny always said I was bossy. I accept that with a smile.

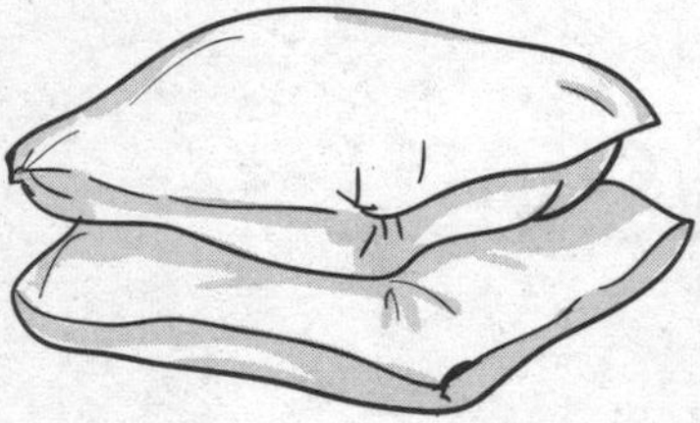

Nighttime pillows are meant to comfort you. If they make your neck hurt, then you need to get rid of them. They really can't be donated. If you hang onto them, they take up a lot of space in your home. I once had a whole cedar chest filled with pillows. I kept them because I had paid a lot of money for them and it felt awful throwing them away. Finally, I did it—and it felt so good to have them out of my home.

Expensive does not necessarily equate to better. One of my favorite pillows was from my sister's home. She had purchased pillows at a discount store for only seven bucks each. I could not believe it. My sweet sister just gave me a pillow.

Do you sleep on your side, back, or tummy? You need more head support if you are on your side. Your pillow must fill the distance from your head to the mattress while keeping your neck straight. A big, fluffy pillow will cradle your head when you sleep on your side. A thin, squishy pillow is good for back and stomach sleepers. You don't want to throw your neck out of alignment.

A great way to try out a pillow is when you are at a hotel. Most hotels pride themselves on having great linens and pillows. Check the tag to find the brand name if you like the one you use. The hotel may have its own exclusive brand, so check with the concierge. You might also be able to purchase pillows from the hotel's website.

On the Fly!

Place your bed pillows in protective covers. These covers are inexpensive and keep your pillows clean. We all know that drool happens, even if we won't admit to it!

PILLOWS FOR DECOR

We can change the look of our living rooms with a few simple pillowcases for throw pillows on the sofa. You don't have to buy the whole pillow. Pillow coverings are easy to sew, too, or not, if you can't sew. For a few dollars' worth of fabric, you can create a new look for your living room. With a simple search on the internet, you can find no-sew pillowcases and make them yourself, nice and easy.

I like to change my couch pillows to lighten up for spring and summer. In the winter, I like holiday pillowcases to make our home look festive or flannel pillowcases to make the room cozier. Such a simple change can make a huge difference in the feeling of the room.

CLEAN YOUR PILLOWS

Pillows need to be freshened up annually. My grandmother would hang them out on the clothesline. Most of us don't have clotheslines any longer, so I put mine in the chairs on my back deck on a breezy day. There is nothing like the smell of a pillow that has been freshened in the wind and sun. If your pillows can be washed and dried, this works, too. You might need to toss some clean tennis shoes or balls in the dryer to beat the pillows as they dry.

A few new pillowcases for your decorative pillows help you do an instant remodel in your home. It is an inexpensive way to refresh your environment.

On the Fly!

Once a year, air out your bed pillows in the sunshine.

THE ISLAND OF MISFIT TEES

The island of misfit tees. You know the place I'm talking about—it's that overflowing drawer you've packed with random tee shirts that you can't wear but won't give away because they remind you of special events, favorite teams, and happy times. No wonder you don't have room to put your clean clothes away. Your precious drawer space has been invaded by squatters.

It's time to live in the here and now, and that means saying goodbye to old and unwearable clothing. You have your memories, and if you need more, take pictures of the tee shirts you

love most. Then, toss the tee, add it to your stash of laundry room cleaning rags, or donate it to a shelter for the dogs and cats to love on. If you're crafty or know someone who is, you can even make a throw blanket out of them. If not, there are plenty of shopkeepers on Etsy who would be happy to do it for you.

Remember, if we kept everything we ever wore, used, or bought, we would need five houses. We are not museum curators. You can do this! Now set your timer, be strong, and have your trash bag and giveaway box handy.

Once you've cleared out those hangers-on, keep your tee shirt drawer lean and mean by discarding one tee shirt every time you bring a new one home. If you really want a gold star, toss out *two* for every one you bring home. When you get really good at this, you'll only buy the tees that you'll really use and enjoy.

Stick with it!
Where to put it:
In your tee shirt drawer
What to write:
Toss a tee or two

THE GREAT SOCK-AND-UNDIE PURGE

I think we can all agree that going commando is generally not an option, and thus we need a fair number of clean underpants at our disposal. Socks and bras, too, are good to have on hand if we intend to leave the house on anything like a regular basis. However, from the state of most of our underwear drawers, it seems like we're outfitting an army of sockless, undie-less, undiscriminating people every day.

Whether you've accumulated all these extras because you've dashed out to buy more instead of doing the laundry or you just can't bear to part with the socks that you wore in college, I'm here to tell you that it's time to let go. You deserve to feel good in your clothes, and that's just as true for the ones that nobody besides you can see.

Let's get those drawers in order. We are going to set our timers for 10 minutes, but it might go even faster.

As you sift through your sock and underwear drawers, ask yourself these questions about each item:

→ Does it fit?

→ Is it comfortable to wear, no itching or poking?

→ Do I like the color?

→ Does it still have its original shape, without being stretched?

→ Is it free of stains?

→ Is it free of holes?

→ Do I feel good when I wear it?

If you answer no to any of the above, toss it. You deserve better. If you have extra socks that are in good condition, set them aside to drop at a homeless shelter for those who need them. Don't donate used underwear.

Next, go through the remaining items and separate the ones you like the most. These are the underpants, camis, tanks, slips, and bras that fit you best and make you feel most confident. Using a notebook, your favorite note-taking app, or just your camera, record the size and brand of these favorites. Next time you need to replace them, you'll be ready to buy exactly what you like. Buy a package to donate, too.

Pretty soon, every item in this drawer will be something you love that makes you feel wonderful.

Now let's get your "keep" pile organized. It's hard for a drawer to stay tidy when it's filled with lots of light, little things, which is why I keep these items in a flat wicker basket in my bathroom. They are readily available when I am getting dressed in the morning. I fold them and place them in the basket vertically like files in a file folder. This way I can grab the color I want without disturbing the whole pile.

Any time I acquire new ones, I seize the opportunity to eliminate any old stained ones. My husband has a fun system that he uses when we travel. He takes his oldest underwear and discards them in the trash while we are on the trip. No more dirty underwear in his suitcase, and he comes home to decluttered drawers. Isn't he brilliant?

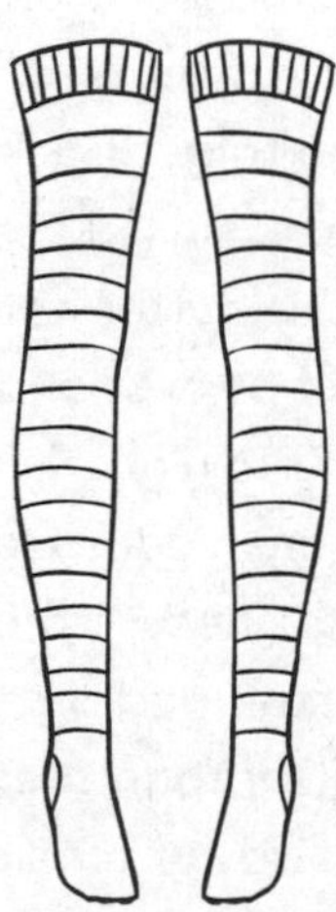

EXTINGUISH YOUR HOT SPOTS

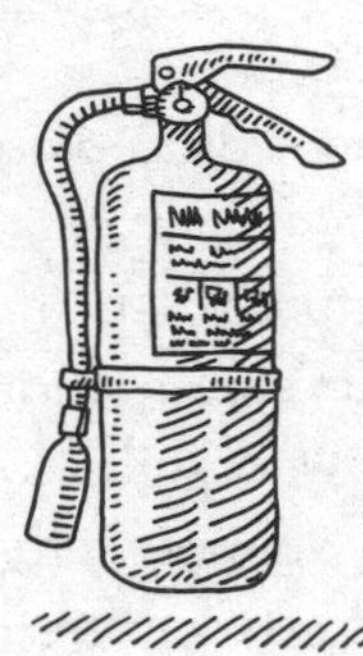

Hot Spots are places where we allow ourselves to procrastinate by plopping odds and ends instead of putting them where they belong. You know where to find your Hot Spots—look for the places where you drop everything when you get home from work or when you're rushing to get out the door in the morning. Maybe it's your kitchen counter, entryway table, or living room chair. I once had a rocking chair piled so high that it tipped over from all the coats I had thrown over the back.

We have become immune to clutter. It is as if we have blinders on. We don't see our clutter as clutter; we look at it as a project that we are going to get back to, or we don't see it at all because we've gotten too used to its presence as a fixture in our homes. You know this clutter well. It's been attacking you for years. It piles up and tips over and ends up on the floor. It trips you in the middle of the night.

Sometimes Hot Spots are hidden from the eye—filling up our drawers, cabinets, closets, sheds, storage units, and the trunks of our cars. We stuff the stuff and then forget about it. Hidden Hot Spots aren't any better than the ones in plain sight, and in fact they're just a gateway to public Hot Spots: Once you've filled every nook and cranny, you're forced to move on to open spaces, such as the basement, to dump your belongings.

Clutter is stressful, and it's self-inflicted. We've all heard the defenses and excuses: *I work better under pressure. I know where everything is even if no one else does. A clear desk is an empty head*. But those are just pretty spins on stressful messes, so let them go and embrace the peace that comes from a clear space.

Our perfectionism causes us to procrastinate. We tell ourselves we don't have time. What we really mean is that we don't have time to do it right. From the day we came into this world, we have been told that if we can't do it perfectly, we shouldn't do it at all. That's a load of hooey.

Every room has a Hot Spot or two. Even your car can be a rolling Hot Spot. Where are yours? Look around your home, especially in these areas:

KITCHEN

- → Kitchen island
- → Dining table
- → End of the counter

LIVING ROOM

- → Coffee table
- → End table
- → Back of a chair

CAR

- → Backseat
- → Trunk
- → Passenger seat
- → Floor

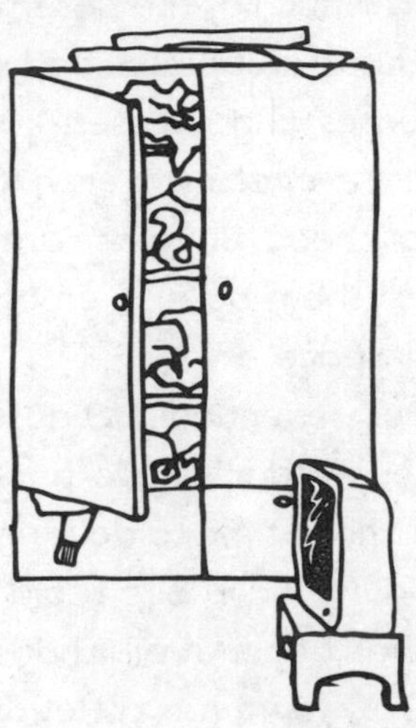

ENTRYWAY

- → Bench
- → Table

BEDROOM

- → Dresser
- → Nightstand
- → Treadmill
- → Chair

BATHROOM

- → Counter
- → Sides of the tub
- → Back of the commode
- → Hamper

2

Once you've mapped your Hot Spots, it's time to get to work. Take 2 minutes and focus on one Hot Spot at a time. In 2 minutes, I want you to

→ Gather everything in the Hot Spot in a basket.

→ Take the basket to another room.

→ One by one, put away as many items as you can in their proper places. If something doesn't have a home, find one. You're the only one who can decide where it should go.

→ Put a sticky note o n the Hot Spot to prevent future clutter.

Eliminating Hot Spots is only half the job—we also have to be vigilant about preventing new ones from popping up. When you're tempted to leave an item where it doesn't belong, catch yourself and put it away properly. You'll thank yourself later when you wake up each day to a tidy home.

Stick with it!
Where to put it:
On any Hot Spot
What to write:
Stop the Hot Spot!

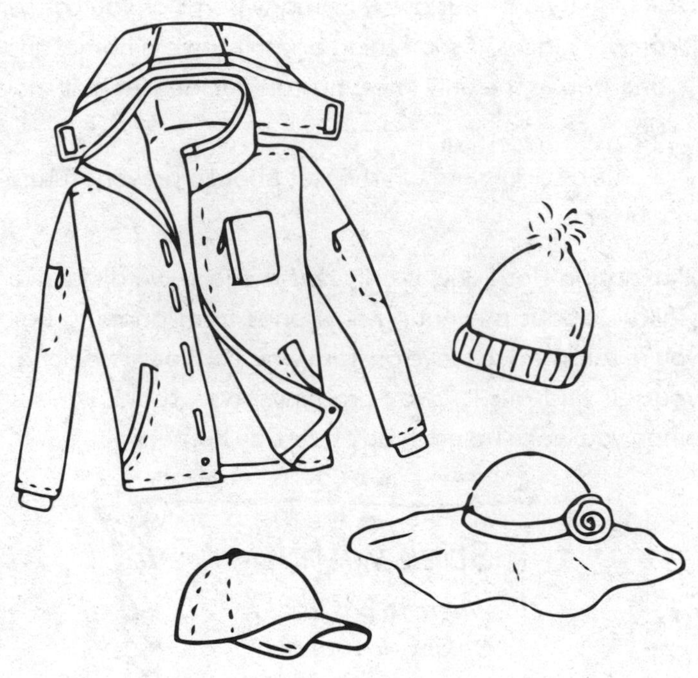

CONQUER THE COAT CLOSET

Jackets, windbreakers, parkas, fleeces, wraps, puffers, trenches. We have all kinds of coats for all kinds of weather, and we have them in various colors, sizes, and dressiness levels. If we aren't careful, our coats will fill our closets until they're so tightly sardined we can barely see what's in there.

Let's take a 5-minute dive into that coat closet. See anything you haven't worn in the last year? How about two if last year's weather was especially mild? If you haven't worn something in that time, chances are you won't wear it again. While those coats are languishing in your closet, they could be helping a family in need of protection and warmth. Steel yourself, pull out those coats, and prepare to donate. Before you do, though, comb carefully through the pockets for stashed dollar bills, that bracelet you've been looking for, or other hidden treasures. Then put the coats in a box and whisk it right out to your car. It does not belong in your home! If it's in your car, you'll be all set to drop it off at a donation station or Salvation Army.

Behold the beauty of your newly curated coat closet.

On the Fly!

Put a vertical row of hooks inside the closet to neatly store hats and scarves.

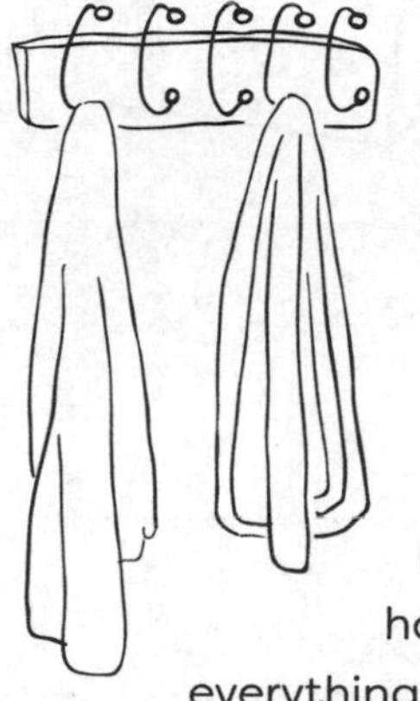

HOOK IT UP

I guess you could say I am addicted to hooks. They are just so handy! They give everything a place and keep everything in its place. Isn't it nice to know exactly where to look to find what you need?

There are all kinds of hooks, for all kinds of walls and uses:

- → Command hooks (easy to remove without damaging walls)
- → Over-the-door hooks
- → Wreath hooks
- → Brick hooks (they grip to the edges of bricks in mortar)
- → Screw-in cup hooks
- → Coat hooks
- → Hat hooks

- → Picture-hanging hooks
- → Pegs for hooks
- → Shower curtain hooks
- → Key hooks
- → Carabiner hooks
- → Purse hooks
- → Over-the-shower-door hooks
- → Bicycle hooks
- → Tool hooks
- → Water hose hooks
- → Velcro (my favorite hook)
- → Kitchen utensil hooks
- → Pot hooks
- → Lantern hooks
- → Bird feeder hooks

Try them for yourself around your house:

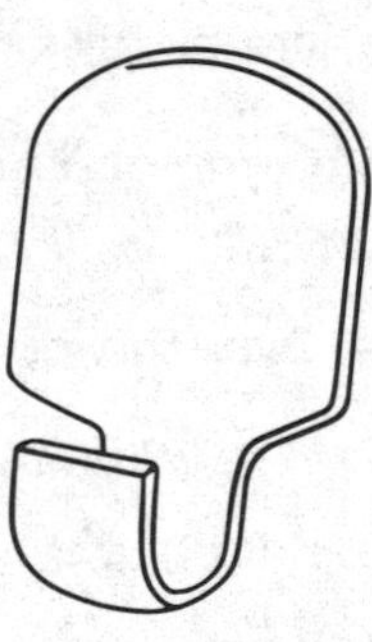

- → Put a hook on your front door to hold a wreath or seasonal decoration.
- → Put a hook on your Launch Pad (see page 90) for totes, coats, and keys.
- → Put a hook on an outside wall to hang a wind chime.
- → Put a brick hook by your fireplace to hang fireplace tools.

→ Put a command hook on the side of your end table to hold charging cords.

→ Put a command hook by your back door to hang binoculars or a flashlight.

Hooks are especially helpful in the kitchen. Give these spots a try:

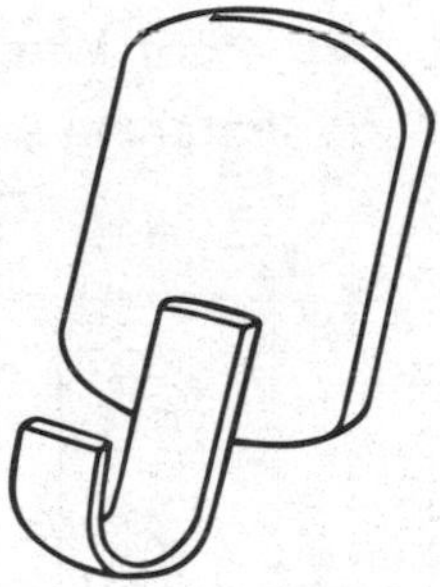

→ Under the kitchen sink to hold your Rubba tools and a purple rag

→ On the inside of cabinet doors by the stove to hold pot holders

→ Outside of your trash can to hold the liner bag in place

→ In the pantry to hang pots and lids

The bathroom is a super spot, too:

→ In the shower to hold back scrubbers and loofahs

→ On the wall to hold necklaces and jewelry while you're showering

→ Inside the cabinet door to hold a purple rag for Swish and Swipe

→ Over the door to hang towels, nightclothes, or the outfit you'll be putting on after your shower

In your bedroom, give these a try:

→ Over the door to hold scarves

→ On the side of your nightstand for cell phone chargers

- → Inside your bed frame to hold wires for an electric blanket
- → Command Velcro picture hangers to hang artwork

You can even use them in your tote bags and purses—I have a carabiner on my purse to attach my keys to when I get out of the car. When my hands are full, the last thing I need is to go searching for my keys in every little pocket. Just hook it up!

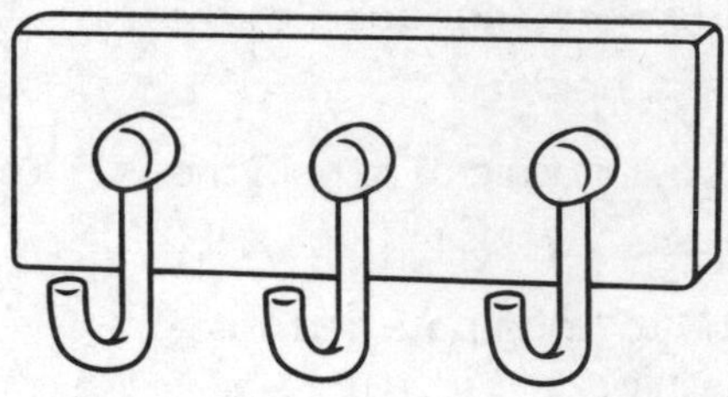

ON A MISSION IN THE KITCHEN

The kitchen is where life at home really takes place. It is where you make your famous cinnamon rolls, help the kids with homework, pay bills, and sip that perfect cup of morning coffee. When your kitchen is a mess, it limits the joy you feel when you're there—and that's too big a loss to take lightly! If you're like many people now whose kitchens are open to the living and dining rooms, that discomfort can seep into the rest of your home, too.

REFRIGERATOR

This may sound obvious, but I'll say it anyway because it's easy to forget: As the space for your family's healthy food, the refrigerator needs to be clean. If it's filled with science projects and defunct condiment jars, it's time for a quick cleanout. Fill your sink with hot soapy water and go through one shelf or drawer at a time. Grab a compost bin or a big plastic bag and empty the science projects and contents of outdated bottles and jars into it. Put the dishes in the sink and rinse the jars and bottles and place them in your recycle bin, or repurpose them if you need containers. (You can soak off those ugly labels and they'll look great!) Load up your dishwasher and wipe down the refrigerator's shelves and drawers.

On the Fly!

Don't use the refrigerator drawers for vegetables because they get forgotten and turn to slime in there. We use ours for drinks, cheeses, bacon, and extra butter. Your vegetables need to be in view so you use them in a timely fashion.

STOVE

We've gotten the rest of the kitchen in pretty good shape, and now the stove is calling our name. Put the drip pan in the dishwasher or hot soapy water and then use a little window cleaner and sponge to wipe down the surface of your stove. Now, don't let your perfectionism keep you at this for hours. As we say in the South, this is hitting a lick at a snake. In other words, just do something. If your stove has been dirty for a long time, it's not going to get clean in a day—but it will begin to look better. Right now we're just going for removing one layer of cooked-on grime. I didn't tell you to clean the oven, either. At the moment, we're just focusing on surface dirt.

On the Fly!

If you have a smooth-surface cooktop, you can use a single-edge razor blade to remove the unsightly burnt-on rings. If your stove is gas, put regular grates in the dishwasher. If you have cast-iron grates, they will rust in the dishwasher and then need to be seasoned, which is a whole shebang, so just soak them in hot water and soap until the goo gets soft and you can easily scrub it off.

Stick with it!
Where to put it:
By the sink
What to write:
A shiny sink = a happy home

SINK

If your sink is full of dirty dishes, empty your sink by setting them on the counter. The 15-minute mission is not to wash the dishes but to shine the sink itself. Take cleanser and a scouring pad, put on a song you like, and scrub, scrub, scrub. If there's gunk around the edges, then scrape it with the point of a knife. Use an old toothbrush to scrub around the faucets, and then rinse the whole thing well. Next, use window cleaner to polish it. Even with the dishes piled on the counter, that shiny sink is going to make your day. Practice keeping your sink shiny from now on by drying it with a dish towel each time you clean it. Keeping it shiny is so easy after you spend these 15 minutes getting it that way. It just takes a wipe.

DISHWASHER

Here's the dirt on dishwashers: Some of us (you know who you are) don't empty the dishwasher until the dirty dishes are piled high in the sink. Just how long does it take, anyway, to empty your dishwasher and put away the dishes? Set your timer and see for yourself.

From now on, make a habit of emptying the dishwasher as soon as it finishes running. That way, you will never again have to see a dirty dish in your shining sink.

COUNTERS

Are your kitchen countertops covered with appliances you don't use? Start at one end of the counters and clear off anything that doesn't need to be there. Put unused appliances in deep storage or give them away. Work as fast as you can so you can quickly experience the thrill of seeing all that beautiful open space. After this, you'll never want to keep another appliance on the counter unless you use it at least twice a week. Think of it this way: Each appliance has to earn a place of honor on your counter.

Do one thing at a time and stay focused. We are not cleaning out cabinets to find a place to put things. If you have to, just put them in the bottom of a closet or in the garage for the time being. Designate one specific workspace on the counter for making coffee, baking, and prepping vegetables.

Got Kids? ***Don't put your cleaning supplies under the sink without a safety lock on the cabinet doors!***

UNDER THE SINK

Grab a trash bag and prepare to enter the netherworld. We're going to toss out those empty glass jars and vases, dirty dish rags, and ancient cleaning supplies. Pick up an item, toss it in the trash, put it in a box to give away, or pack it up to put away someplace else. This space needs to be open so you can tell if there's a leak in the plumbing.

Only keep scouring pads, dishwasher detergent, liquid dish soap, paper towels, a cleanser, and window cleaner under here.

As we've learned, soap is soap and it doesn't take a magic potion to clean. We've been fooled for too long by those ads that say we can't clean unless we have their product. Truth be known, most of those products contain nothing more than a little detergent and colored water.

On the Fly!

Stand up cookie sheets, platters, cooking racks, baking pans, and roasting pans on their sides in a cabinet like books on a shelf. A couple of tension rods mounted vertically can help you make a divider. That way, you never have to lift a stack of other things to get to the item you need—you can just slide it out.

POTS AND PANS

When you open your cabinet doors, do pots and pans come tumbling out? Do you have a hard time finding the pan you want to use? Do you think you may have too many in there, anyway? Get ready to pitch some pots and pans.

My stove has four burners, which means that the most I can use are four pots at one time. I have a pasta pot, a 1-quart pot, a 1½-quart pot, and a 2-quart pot. Then I use an iron skillet and a cast-iron Dutch oven. That's it, and I've never needed more. None of my pots needs to be nested inside another one.

So get rid of that cookware set you got when you went to college, and the set that you got when Aunt Harriet died. Keep just what you use and love, and pass along the rest to someone who might use it. Take 15 minutes and purge this cluttered cabinet. Your toes will thank you, as will your aching back because you'll never have to search for a pot again.

Got Kids? Put child-friendly cups and dishes in a lower cabinet so they're easy for little hands to help themselves. This also makes it easy for kids to set the table without your help.

DISHES

2 Are your mismatched dishes, assorted glasses, and plastic cups taking over more cabinet space than they should? If an item isn't used often or doesn't make you smile, it needs to find its way to the trash can. Set your timer for two minutes and start with only one shelf. Just how many dishes do you need, anyway? Here's how many: enough to set the table for one or two meals for your family and the occasional guests, not enough for a whole week!

Pretty dishes can make setting the table a joy, and buying them is affordable when you only get what you need instead of stocking the cabinets from top to bottom. I grant you permission to get rid of those cracked cups and chipped glasses and to find tableware that you love. Baby steps start with getting rid of the old yucky ones. Hey, you may have to eat off your china for a while! (Imagine making every day a holiday and treating yourself like company.)

PANTRY

Is finding something in your pantry a scavenger hunt? The pantry might need a pick-me-up. When we unload our groceries from the car, it's easy to just stash things in the general area of where they should go. Every so often, we need to take an inventory to see what we really do have and make sure we're not accidentally buying duplicates.

Keep your trash can nearby, and if you find mice droppings, you will also need a mask and rubber gloves. Start with one shelf at a time, and don't pull everything out at once. I mean it. If the job seems to be overwhelming, start with baby steps; you don't have to finish the whole pantry in these 10 minutes. It will still be there when you are ready to come back to it. In the meantime, that one clean shelf is going to make you happy.

On the Fly!

If you have special items in your china cabinet that have a history in your family, write notes on a notecard about what makes a piece special and place the card with it.

SILVERWARE

Let's do a silverware sweep. Have you ever wondered how all those crumbs get in this drawer? I know how: We don't close the drawer after we open it. This is an easy fix, and you know the drill by now!

Set all the clean flatware on the counter and wash out the divider tray. Then get rid of anything that does not belong in this drawer, which can often be a go-to spot for your Stash and Dashes. Just think how inspired you'll be the next time you reach for a spoon!

On the Fly!

If you don't have a pantry, clear out a linen closet to use for your food storage. If your pantry (or linen-closet-turned-pantry) has deep shelves, use clear or labeled bins as drawers. Put the newest items toward the back.

DRAWER DEJUNKING

5

Every kitchen has a catchall drawer that becomes the default place to stash anything that doesn't have a real home. Here you'll find tools, nails, batteries, string, hooks, screws, furniture pads, and many other odds and ends. Set your timer for 5 minutes and see how much you can toss, repurpose, or relocate.

CHINA CABINET

5

Do you really love all the china, crystal, and other special serving dishes that you have in your china cabinet? Set your timer for 5 minutes and remove any items you don't like or use. I know this can be hard if you have lots of heirloom pieces. Keep in mind that you can't hold on to everything. If it's all you can do, just pull out one item to give away. Maybe someone else in your family will love it.

RECYCLING STATION

Once you've eliminated the clutter in your cabinets, you'll have space to create a recycling station tucked out of sight. Mine is a cabinet with three bins to sort plastic, glass, and cans. To keep your trash area sanitary, make it a point to immediately empty a bin whenever it is full. Keep the roll of liners in the bottom of the bin or next to it so they are easy to replace. Rinse or wash containers before you put them into the recycling bin to safeguard against odors and discourage insects.

On the Fly!

Put small bins or even an old muffin pan in your drawers to divide them into handy compartments. Line the drawer with a flat piece of cardboard, and tape down the containers to keep them from sliding around when you open and close the drawer.

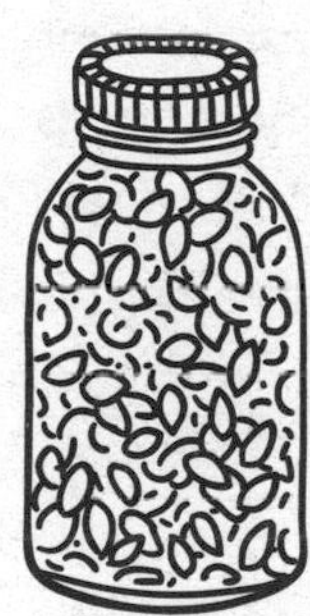

WHERE HAVE YOU BIN ALL MY LIFE?

Jars, Boxes, and Other Containers

Many years ago, I loved to can fruits and vegetables in **mason jars.** The beautiful, clear, inexpensive jars were filled with wholesome food and stored in my pantry. It made me smile to see all this food shining through the glass. I could easily see what was in the jars just by looking, and each lid was dated so I could track the age of the contents. It was an efficient way to store food. Most people don't preserve their own food these days, but we can still transfer store-bought food to clear jars—they look so much better than food packages wrapped in ugly labels printed with marketing slogans.

Those glass jars still make me happy. I thought that I wanted to put all my baking ingredients in one-gallon glass jars. I started collecting them, and my baker's rack filled with glass jars of every shape and size. Eventually, I decided to acquire some **uniform rectangular canisters** to put in a drawer shelf where I usually assemble my recipes. With a label on the top of the hinged lid of a transparent plastic canister, I could easily scoop out ingredients without having to pull out the canister. My counters were not cluttered, and cleanup was a breeze.

On the Fly!

Take your products out of their packaging as soon as you get home. A roll of paper towels looks much calmer, cleaner, and neater when it's not wrapped in plastic that's screaming "new and improved" or "softer than ever!"

My kitchen does have a few canisters out, but they are functionally decorative: a set of red ceramic canisters holds our whole-bean coffee and ground coffee, and a set of clear glass canisters holds granola, dried fruit, and nuts. The best containers are the ones that stack nicely, that can be used in the oven, and that can transfer to the refrigerator later.

For storage outside of the kitchen, large **plastic bins** with lids are terrific and inexpensive. I use colored bins to help me know at a glance what's inside—for instance, my Christmas decorations are stored in red and green bins. If you prefer a cleaner look, you can buy bins all in the same color and label them clearly.

Banker's boxes are helpful for organizing paper clutter. They stack nicely and can be disposed of easily when it is time to get rid of them. Check with your CPA or do an internet search to keep up with the current recommendations on how long to keep papers.

If you need something contained out in the open, consider a piece of **wood furniture.** I have a cedar chest at the foot of our bed that was made by my husband's uncle for Robert's mother as a wedding present. We inherited it and treasure this piece of furniture. It contains an extra blanket and pillows and functions as a cozy place to sit to put on shoes and for the cat to curl up. I really like furniture that doubles as storage—wooden crates can be decorative and functional for storage of heavy items such as vinyl albums and cans of surplus food. Vintage crates can become shelves when they are mounted to walls, and they are great for towel storage or even extra toilet paper.

On the Fly!

See-through storage containers help you know what is inside when you forget to label them.

Wicker baskets add texture to your storage. My printer station is an old repurposed table with a couple of shelves. I also use wicker baskets for drawers: They hold my printer paper, print cartridges, office supplies, and FlyLady memorabilia. In our living room we have wicker baskets with lids for dog treats and fire starters; decorative and functional.

Metal containers are helpful in various ways. I have a metal trash can where we store fireplace ashes until we can dispose of them in the woods. Other metal containers store surplus food. I purchased these six-gallon containers at our local hardware store and filled them with rice, noodles, grits, flour, beans, and other dry items. They keep out moisture and the little four-legged creatures that can chew through almost anything. When you need to protect things, metal cans will do the trick.

On the Fly!

Clear out a section of your bottom cabinets for your canisters.

I have several **cloth containers**, too. They are similar to the fabric storage containers typically used for protecting china and crystal, and they can slide under beds for hidden storage. My favorite cloth storage containers are the colorful fabric drawers for bookcases. They add texture and accent to a room without costing a lot of money. If you are crafty, you could even make your own with cardboard boxes, colored fabric, and some spray adhesive or glue. These can be simple storage for children's toys or your stash of craft supplies.

I love to keep a supply of **brown craft shopping bags with handles.** I can use them to store paper trash that can be burned in my fireplace. They also help me declutter. I grab a bag and run through the house to gather up items to give or throw away. In a pinch, I even use them for gifts—they look great and easily contain odd-sized items. Add some tissue paper and you can turn a plain craft bag into a gift bag.

There is one problem with containers. As you declutter, you will not need as many and you will have to find new uses for the empty ones. Be creative! They can be turned into tables for toddlers, bathtubs for babies, and—my favorite—gardens to grow mushrooms.

On the Fly!

Color-code your holiday decoration storage containers to match the holiday color.

PERFECTLY IMPERFECT COOKING (Plus: Pancakes!)

We've all seen the saying circulating online that the best way to keep the kitchen clean is not to cook at all. That is so sad! You and your family deserve home-cooked meals. Start with a tidy kitchen (see page 73) and then just clean up as you go. When we clear away the competing obstacles of a messy kitchen and our own fear of failure (perfectionism), the kitchen becomes the heart of the home it's really meant to be.

If that's not enough to convince you, let the money do the talking. Let's say you want to make pancakes for your family of four. An egg and a little flour, oil, sugar, and milk—add it up, and it's all less than a dollar or two. But go out for pancakes? That's twenty dollars. Perfectionism wastes money. Not a "good cook"? Who cares? So what if you burn a pancake? Or three? I've learned that the first pancake is always the ugliest, and our dogs get the prize.

YouTube is filled with quick and easy recipes for everything you can think of. Pick something simple you'd like to have, do a search for a *quick and easy* recipe for it, and then watch just one video—don't look for the best! (There's that perfectionism again.) Before you know it, you'll have more confidence in the kitchen and your own signature lineup of simple go-to meals that you can make in your sleep. (For help with menu planning and tips on stocking the pantry to set yourself up for success, see page 80.)

To get you started, here's my no-fail pancake recipe.

FLYLADY'S PERFECTLY IMPERFECT PANCAKES

1. Pull out all the ingredients, bowls, and utensils.

2. Turn on oven to 200 degrees to keep pancakes warm after you cook them.

3. Turn your griddle or skillet on medium high heat before you start mixing the batter.

4. You don't need a mixer—just use a fork to mix together 1 cup milk, 2 eggs, 2 Tbsp sugar, 1½ cups self-rising flour, and 2 tsp oil or melted butter. I keep powdered milk as a backup for recipes.

5. Stir until all ingredients are just mixed together. The thicker the batter, the fatter the pancake.

6. To check for the proper griddle temperature, wet your finger and put a drop in the hot skillet; if it dances around, the skillet is hot enough.

7. Use the ⅓ cup to scoop the batter into the pan, or recycle a large ketchup bottle to squeeze the batter directly into the pan.

8. Little air bubbles will start to form in the batter. When the pancake is lightly covered with tiny bubbles, it is time to flip it. If the pancakes look too dark, adjust the temperature.

9. Allow each pancake to cook for a few more minutes, then put them on a plate in the warmed oven until all the batter is cooked.

10. Freeze extra pancakes to have for breakfast later in the week.

Serve with your favorite syrup, butter, whipped cream, or jam. If you like, you can try adding blueberries, banana slices, or chocolate chips to the batter. You'll be a pancake ace.

Here's another secret: Pancake batter made just a little thicker can become muffins; a little thinner, crepes.

On the Fly!

FRIDGE TIPS

→ Put scraps and peelings in your refrigerator in resealable bags. You can see what is in the bag and it makes for easy cleanup. If it is not trash day, mark the bag with a big X and put it in the freezer. Then on trash day throw all the bags of garbage away.

→ Don't use crisper drawers for fresh fruit and veggies. Out of sight, out of mind. Use the drawers to store drinks, cheeses, butter, cream cheese, and other packaged items instead.

→ Use the very last bits from the bottoms of jars of condiments, like jams, jellies, ketchup, BBQ sauce, and salad dressing, by emptying them into your slow cooker with chicken pieces. They'll add flavor and help free up shelf space, and you will have dinner!

→ Stop using refrigerator magnets. They make your refrigerator look cluttered and junky.

→ When you clean out the refrigerator, you may find a few science projects. Bag the spoiled food and freeze it until the night before your trash or compost is ready for pickup—then, put the frozen bag in the bin at the curb. That way you don't have to live with the smell of rotting food.

On the Fly!

TIPS FOR COOKING WITHOUT CHAOS

→ Fill your sink with hot soapy water to soak bowls, measuring cups, utensils, and other items as you go.

→ Start cooking with an empty dishwasher.

→ Put plastic wrap, wax paper, or freezer paper on your counter. This helps with cleanup.

→ Buy self-rising flour; this eliminates the need for baking powder and salt.

→ Clean up spills as they happen by mopping your floor with your feet—use a wet rag or paper towel and go for a skate.

GERM WARFARE

Get Ready for V-Day!

It's a fact that we all need to accept: Germs are a part of life. We can do all we can to protect ourselves from those pesky colds and stomach bugs, but there comes the inevitable day when we wake up with a germ anyway. Despite what big-name disinfectant companies would have us believe, rest assured that a little dirt and dust is actually good for us. Studies show that children who are raised in pristine environments can suffer more from asthma, allergies, and other autoimmune issues. So, if your home isn't perfect, pat yourself on the back!

Here are seven simple precautions that help minimize the spread of harmful germs—especially important during cold and flu season—without killing all the helpful bacteria that keep us healthy.

1. Wash your hands with soap and hot water when you get home, and have your children do the same. A good hand washing should take at least as long as it takes you to sing "Happy Birthday" to yourself from start to finish.

2. At home, dry your hands with white washcloths instead of one communal towel, and toss each cloth in the laundry after use. (I got mine online 12 for $5 and bought four dozen. I keep some by the sink in every bathroom, along with a separate small basket for the dirty ones.)

3. Keep antibacterial cloths in your purse to wipe down shopping cart handles before use. Use these cloths to wipe the steering wheel of your car once a week as well.

4. Use a shirttail or an elbow rather than your hands to push open the doors in public places.

5. Wipe down your phone with alcohol each day, and do the same with light switches and doorknobs once a week.

6. Avoid putting your purse on the floor, and wipe down the exterior once a week or so.

7. Wear indoor shoes. Put the dirty, germy ones in your closet.

It's so important for you to take care of yourself. If you don't take care of you, who will?

Stick with it!
Where to put it:
By your high-traffic light switches
What to write:
Clean me

SAY BYE TO THE BOOKS

Are you a book hoarder? I understand. Books are my passion, too. I love the way they feel in my hands, the way they look on the shelf, and the memories they hold. It makes me happy just knowing they are there, in easy reach whenever I need them. But as much as I love books, I don't love the clutter and dust of books that are no longer earning their place in my home.

My feeling is that books make us feel smart. And that's a good feeling! But sometimes we take it too far, and we cling to our books like they are precious until they take over our homes.

How do you know that you have too many books?

- → Books are everywhere: in piles on the floor, stacked on tabletops, and crammed tightly into shelves.
- → Books are dusty.
- → Books are not organized or easy to find.

→ Books are in boxes that you haven't opened for years.

→ Books are stored in musty places, like basements and sheds.

On the Fly!

Do you have a fund-raiser coming up? Put together a collection of books on a single topic and offer it as an auction item.

Books can become another form of paper clutter. At one time or another, we have all held onto books from our childhood, school days, and early adulthood—not because those books were particularly special to us but because it felt wrong, somehow, to give them away. Could this be another layer of perfectionism that needs to be addressed? Holding on to books for the sake of having them is hoarding.

So, I'm here to tell you that it's time to make a donation. There are plenty of ways those books can be serving a better purpose. Imagine what good they will do in schools, libraries, and Salvation Army stores. You can donate books to be sent

to soldiers overseas or offer them to prisons for rehabilitating inmates (some prisons will accept them; others won't).

The best part is that you don't have to do this all at once. Please don't purge books in a day-long marathon! This is too difficult. Take it slow and steady. Be kind to yourself. Here's how to start:

1. Set your timer for 3 minutes.
2. Stand in front of your bookcase and pick five books to donate.
3. Place those books in a bag and put the bag in your car.
4. Next time you're out, drop them off at a library or any other place that accepts donations.

Do this five days in a row and you'll be amazed at the space you create. And don't stop there—keep going! Remember, a few books a day keeps the dust away.

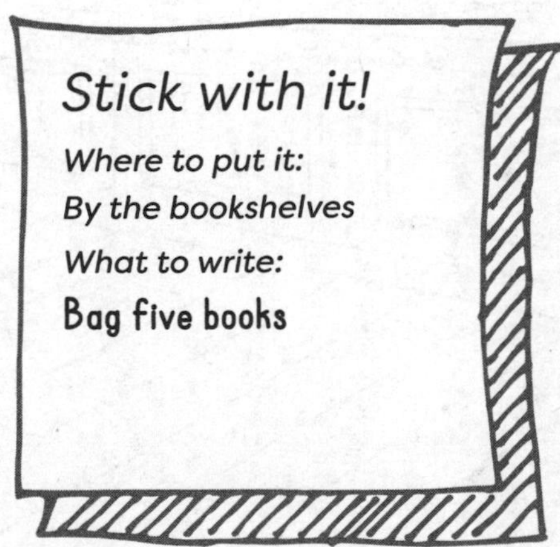

Stick with it!
Where to put it:
By the bookshelves
What to write:
Bag five books

3, 2, 1 . . . LAUNCH!

Where is the funniest place you have found your keys after a hard day at work? One time mine were in the refrigerator. Another time they were in my tinfoil drawer. It took me forever to find them and you can imagine how late I was to work the next day!

That was before I made myself a **Launch Pad**.

A Launch Pad is a place you establish in your home to store the items that you need to get you out the door in the morning. Think about all the hours you've wasted searching for the objects you need to bring with you into the world—not just your keys but also your shoes, your wallet, your tote bag or purse or backpack, a coat, an umbrella. . . .

If just one of these is misplaced, you have to run around the house looking for it. By the time you find it—*if* you find it—you're sweaty, late, and all stressed out.

Instead, if you put those items where they belong when you

get home, you won't have to spend precious time in the morning tearing up the house looking for them. You'll be calm and collected as you leave for your day. That's the way to start your day right.

All you have to do is establish a spot for these items—a Launch Pad—and put it to work. A Launch Pad can be highly designed and customized, with hooks and shelves and cubbies, or it can be a simple basket on the floor by the door. Either way, you need a designated spot for your daily necessities.

On the Fly!

Put your keys on a bright-colored lanyard or carabiner to make them easier to hang and easier to find.

Here are a few ways you can make your Launch Pad work for you:

Use hooks: Put hooks on the wall by the door for your keys, coat, and bag. Try putting them at different levels for different items; long coats should go on higher hooks.

Repurpose furniture: Move a small dresser near your entryway and give each drawer a purpose. Or, if you have a family or roommates, give each person his or her own drawer. A credenza or nightstand will work, too. How about a simple chair?

Borrow a bookcase: Take the books off the shelves and use the shelves for your daily items. You can put bins and baskets on the shelves for smaller objects. Or you can turn the entire bookshelf on its side and create side-by-side cubbies. The top will become a bench you can sit on while putting on your shoes in the morning and taking them off at the end of the day.

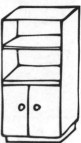

Get a locker: It worked in high school, so why not use one now? You can buy a cheap and trendy locker online in a color of your choice.

Once you have your Launch Pad set up, get your sticky notes out and label the place where each item should go. Everything has a place of its own. With this system, you'll be ready for your day, every day.

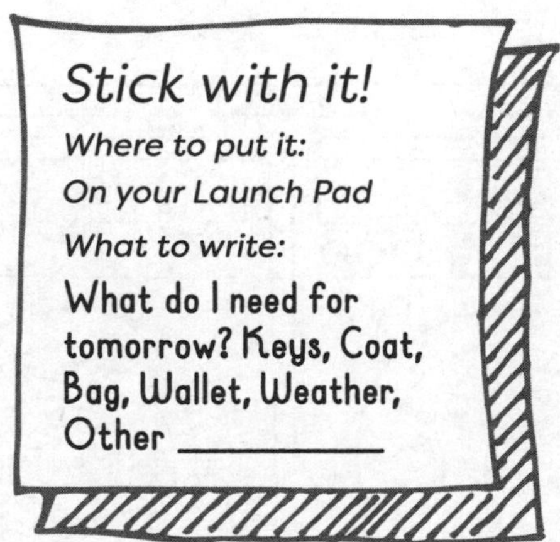

Stick with it!
Where to put it:
On your Launch Pad
What to write:
What do I need for tomorrow? Keys, Coat, Bag, Wallet, Weather, Other ___________

A LIGHTER LOAD

Laundering Lessons

When I was little, laundry was a huge ordeal. My grandmother had an electric wringer washer and a clothesline, and laundry took all day. That didn't even include ironing! Today our modern machines give us a choice: We can make laundry a pain, or we can make it a process.

What makes laundry harder now is that we all have way too many clothes. When my sisters and I were little, each of us had only a few outfits. These days, buying new clothes is so easy and cheap we have too much of a good thing. And when we run out of clean clothes, it is simple to avoid the washing machine by buying something new to wear instead.

Let's first get your laundry system under control. Five simple steps can make doing laundry much easier:

1. Sort
2. Wash
3. Dry
4. Fold or hang
5. Stow

When you skip any of these steps, you create a logjam. And when you have a logjam, you have CHAOS.

SORT

If you don't sort your laundry into types and colors, you'll probably end up with pink-fuzz-covered clothing. Put whites in one pile, darks in another, and brights in a third. While you're sorting, inspect your clothes for stains that will be harder to get out if you don't pretreat them. I'm always making spots on my clothes—when we go out, my friends wait to see how long it will take before I accidently spill food on my chest, which I call "feeding the girls"!

On the Fly!

When you take off your clothes at the end of the day, look for stains and dab them with dishwashing liquid.

The other reason we sort our laundry is to go on a scavenger hunt for money, receipts, tissues, and any other tidbits we've left in our pockets. If you do this every night when you undress, it will make doing the laundry go faster.

On the Fly!

Check the tag before you buy new clothing. If it says "Dry Clean Only," think about whether you really want to commit to that extra errand and expense. (It's easy to ruin an expensive item by accidentally putting it in the washing machine!) For me, I usually skip that purchase unless the item is for a special occasion.

Towels and sheets have to be sorted by color, too. When you purchase towels, washcloths, and sheets, consider sticking with one color to make your cleaning process easier. I like white or a light color because, this way, I can use hot water and bleach or nonbleach whitening detergent.

One of the secrets to sorting is to have separate baskets, bins, or hampers for darks, lights, and brights. If there is room in the place where you tend to change your clothes, keep the bins there. As you undress, you can decide whether an item needs to be washed and, if so, place it in the right basket. When the basket is full, you have a load to wash. If the item can be worn again without washing, hang it up where it belongs right away—no draping clothing over a chair or piling it on your dresser.

WASH

Here is a secret that I have learned only recently: Use the delicate cycle for most of the items you wash. When you pretreat stains, you don't have to wash things so vigorously to get the stains out. The delicate cycle is shorter, and it keeps your clothes looking newer far longer than the regular cycle because it doesn't beat the fabric up or continually remove microscopic amounts of dye until the color is completely different from what you purchased.

Try to do a load a day. Small loads are less overwhelming.

On the Fly!

You don't need a fresh towel every day—but by no means leave it on the floor. Hang up your towel and allow it to dry. This will reduce your laundry CHAOS by minimizing the pile in the laundry basket.

DRY

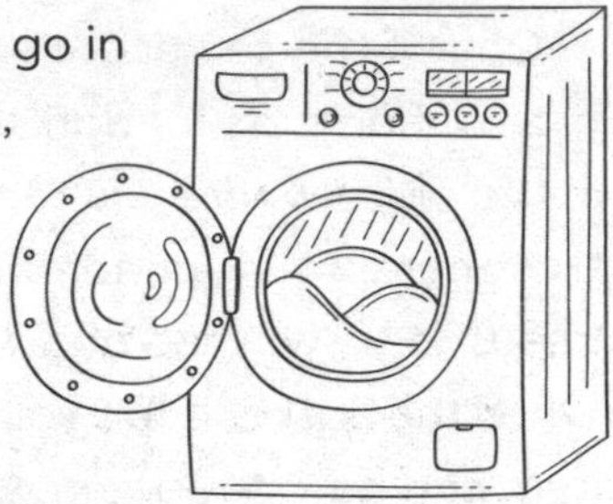

Not every item of clothing needs to go in the dryer. If you wear a lot of cotton, the dryer can shrink those items. Get into the habit of gathering empty clothes hangers and taking them to the laundry with you. Many items can be hung up as you empty the washing machine and given a brisk diagonal tug to smooth out wrinkles while they are wet. This is called blocking, and it often works well enough to allow you to skip ironing once the item is dry. Hang these items to dry in an open area, such as on the shower rod or a door. I have a rod over my washer and dryer for these items. In wintertime, hanging clothes to dry has the added benefit of acting as a humidifier, putting much-needed moisture into your home.

The number one wrench in our laundry works? Procrastination.

Leave a load of laundry to mildew in the washing machine, and you'll see what I mean. Ditto on the cold, wrinkled clothing that's been left too long in the dryer. Understanding yourself is half the battle of doing laundry. I set a timer to keep my mind focused. Most machines have a buzzer to remind you, but my washer and dryer are in the basement, so I often do not hear the buzz to alert me.

The dryer needs your undivided attention, so stay focused. This is not as important when towels and sheets are being dried. Never leave the house or go to sleep with the dryer running. Many house fires start because of lint-filled dryer vents. It's essential to have a working smoke alarm near your laundry area and a fire extinguisher handy.

FOLD OR HANG

Then either fold clothing or hang it up. Most of your good clothing needs to go on hangers. As you hang items in your closet, you can put whole outfits together. This makes picking out clothes for tomorrow easier. As for your workout clothes, they can be folded together in pairs, with a top and yoga pants in one neat little bundle.

On the Fly!

There's no wrong way to fold! The only wrong way to fold is to stuff the clothing into a laundry basket so those wrinkles can settle in.

On the Fly!

Less is more when it comes to your clothing. Every time you put clothing away, grab a few items to donate. Take them to your car so you can drop them off when you're out. Your closet will thank you!

STOW

Now for the most important part: putting it away. We're all guilty of having lived out of a laundry basket. Even if laundry is folded all nice and neat, eventually everything is wrinkled because you're snatching things out of the basket one by one. If you have a pet, then you know the dangers of leaving a basket full of clean laundry on the floor. It becomes their favorite (fur-covered) place to sleep. If your critter is mad at you, you might even get a present.

To make it easier to put your clothing away, free up space in your closet. Too many clothes make life harder and get in the way of your routines.

There are a couple of ways to organize the clothing in your closet.

Option 1

Put like items together: tanks, short-sleeved shirts, long-sleeved shirts, dresses, skirts, pants, and so forth. If you like, you can divide them by color within each section.

Option 2

Put whole outfits together. I put a top with a pair of pants, hang both hangers inside of the shirt, and drape a scarf around it. I especially like to do this when I travel, so I know I'll have exactly what I need.

Whichever method you choose I want you to love everything you have and wear it regularly.

Here is one more tip for you: At the beginning of the season, turn all the hangers backward in your closet. When you put your clothes away after doing laundry, put them in the closet the correct way. This way, you'll be able to see what you haven't worn, and after a few months you can either get rid of those items or put them together into outfits that you'll really wear.

When you have a system for doing your laundry and keeping it done, your life will be better and more spontaneous all around. It'll be easier to grab some clothes and head out on a weekend trip with friends without even having to do laundry. Your mornings will be less stressful, too—no more rushing to find something to wear! You will know what you have, and you'll be wearing what you love.

On the Fly!

A load of laundry each day keeps the laundry lament away. Toss one load in after dinner, move it to the dryer the next morning, then fold and put away; repeat after dinner.

TO IRON OR NOT TO IRON

As a child, I watched my grandmother sprinkle clothes with water, roll them up, then place them in the refrigerator. I never really knew why. Laundry was a huge, all-day affair. It started early in the morning with her treasured wringer washer. That wringer put a lot of creases in the clothes. My granny had many steps to her wash day: sort, wash, wring, rinse, wring, hang on the clothesline, take off the clothesline, fold, sprinkle, roll up, put in the refrigerator, iron, and put away.

We are so thankful to have appliances that do most of the work for us. What's up with ironing? We hate it, but we like to look nice in smooth clothes. So we iron.

The reason we have to iron is because we have created the wrinkles in our clothing with our own procrastination and being in a hurry. How could that be?

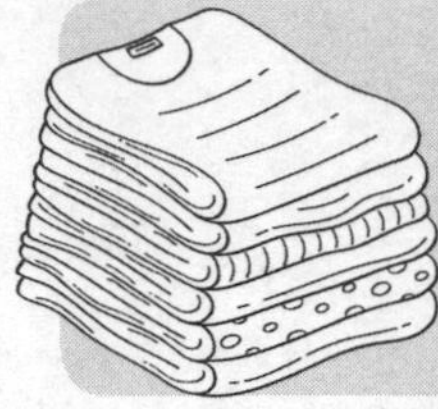

On the Fly!

Check tags on clothes before you buy. If they say "Dry Clean Only," you may want to make another choice.

1. The washing machine is filled to the maximum capacity. After all, if we stuff more clothes in, it makes for fewer loads to wash.

2. We use only one cycle on our washing machines: Regular. Didn't read the owner's manual!

3. Then we let clothing **sit** in the washer after it finishes.

4. We dry the clothes on hot so they finish quickly.

5. Then we let them **sit** in the cold dryer after it finishes.

6. We drag them out of the dryer and into a laundry basket.

7. Then we let them **sit** in the basket.

8. Then we are forced to **iron**!

With a few simple changes to our inefficient laundry routine, we can cut out the need for ironing. We abuse our clothing. It is expensive, and we need to treat it with a delicate hand.

1. Wash fewer clothes at one time.

2. Wash on delicate; the spin cycle is not violent and creates fewer wrinkles.

3. Take clothes out of the washer.

4. Some clothes do not need to be dried in the dryer: undergarments last longer when allowed to air-dry.

5. Stretch each piece side to side (blocking) to smooth out wrinkles with your hand and hang it up to dry or shake each piece to release the spin wrinkles and put it in the dryer.

6. Set your dryer on delicate; a lower heat setting does not set the wrinkles.

7. Don't allow the dryer to finish and stop. Open the door, allow the drum to stop turning, grab an item of clothing, then restart the dryer while you hang the piece up. Do this till everything is folded or hung up.

8. Now if you need to iron, it will only be to touch up collars and buttons. I have ironed my linen tops right out of the washer when they were still wet. Linen only looks nice for a few minutes after you put it on.

On the Fly!

Do a load of laundry each day from start to finish. You will not feel rushed. It's just one load.

When you do need to iron your clothing so that it looks good, examine why it needs to be ironed and commit to making some changes.

1. Was it in a crammed closet?
2. Did your folding create more wrinkles?
3. Was it trapped in a suitcase while traveling?
4. Did you pull it out of a cold dryer or laundry basket?

5. Has it been sat on because it was piled on the sofa?

6. Do you want creases in your jeans or sleeves?

On the Fly!

Don't leave your ironing board and iron out all the time. Pets and children—and *you*—can knock it over and get hurt or burned. And if your iron hits the floor, you will be buying a new one. They are expensive.

Now that you know how to *not iron,* here's how to do it when you've gotta:

Throw the piece of clothing back in the dryer for a few minutes. My favorite way.

Or . . .

1. Drag out your ironing board and iron.

2. Put on a good movie.

3. Check the tag on the clothing to see the iron temperature.

4. Wet a dishtowel to help protect the fabric from an iron that is too hot, even if you have a steam iron.

5. Start with the hard parts first: collars, buttons, sleeves, and shoulders.

6. Then do the body.

7. For pants with creases, match the seams to find the center and then iron. Or there is a tool that you can buy on Amazon called a pants stretcher. Our grandparents used them to dry creases into their pants.

8. Then hang it up. If you have trouble hanging your clothes in your closet, it is time to declutter to make room for your clothing to hang freely.

On the Fly!

When you buy an iron, make sure it turns itself off automatically.

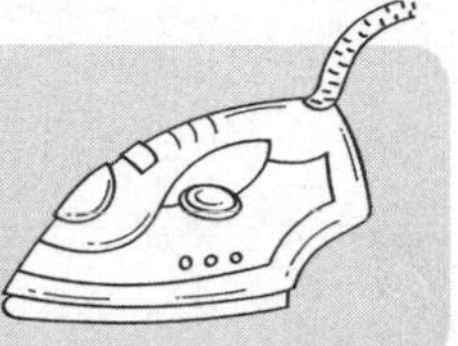

Ironing is usually the result of procrastination on our part. If you still like your clothes to have a crisp, freshly ironed look, then by all means iron. Make ironing part of your before-bed routine to get your clothes ready for tomorrow. There is nothing like getting up in the morning to your whole outfit picked out and ready to put on, with no need to drag out the ironing board and be rushed to get ready for your day.

Stick with it!
Where to put it:
By your hamper
What to write:
A load a day keeps
Mount Washmore away

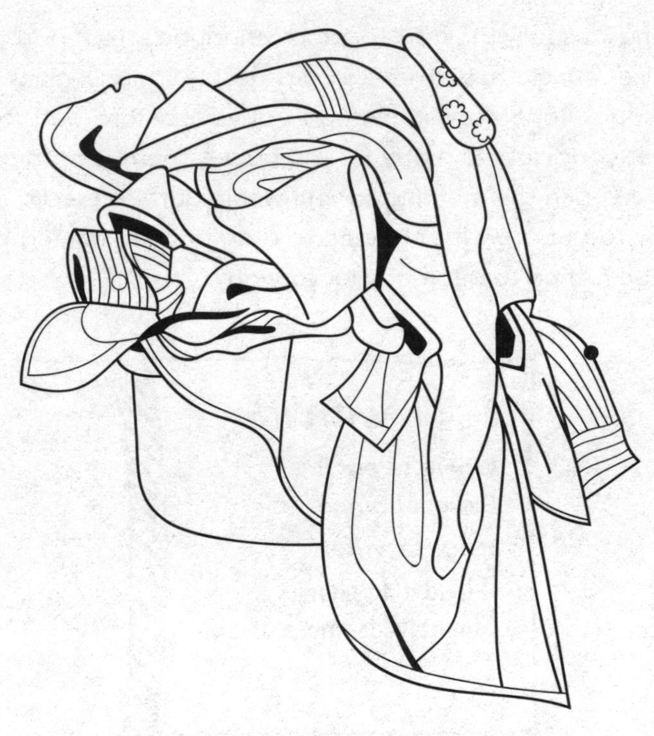

LIBERATE YOUR LINEN CLOSETS

Linen closets are a great way to keep things you don't need. When you buy new sheets and towels, do you get rid of the old ones? I didn't think so. Your linen closet is probably chockful of extras that are taking up space and making mountains of mess. Get rid of most of it and you'll be able to find what you want when you want it.

Today, set your timer for 15 minutes because it's time to overhaul this clutter catcher.

1. **Purge old towels.** Get rid of those poor, ratty wretches and send them to the humane society for the puppies and kitties. Leave a few for cleaning up the major messes, but don't keep them here in the linen closet—store them with your cleaning

supplies. Have two or three sets of towels per person in the home. That gives you enough in case your washing machine breaks down. A set of towels comes with a bath towel, hand towel, and washcloth.

2. **Move the washcloths.** Washcloths are used in the bathroom, so move them there. I keep a small basket full of white ones on my bathroom counter for hand drying, face washing, and sink shining. I have four dozen, which I purchased for a few dollars. The white ones can be bleached and washed in hot water, and they give my bathroom a spa feel. I keep a second basket beside the first for tossing the dirty cloths after each use, a nice way to keep us from spreading germs.

3. **Move the hand towels, too.** Hand towels are a great size for pat-drying hair. At the beauty salon that is the size they use.

4. **Toss tired sheets.** Get rid of sheets that are old, mismatched, or faded. Is that most of them? That's fine. Just how many sets of sheets do you need, anyway? I know the answer: two sets for each bed that you have, and an extra set for making up the couch if you have guests. I store the sheets in the room where they are used, either in a bottom drawer or folded flat underneath the mattress.

With that done, consider this radical idea: You don't even really need a linen closet. You've already moved the smaller towels and washcloths to the bathroom, where they belong.

You can keep your extra set of sheets folded flat between the mattress and the box spring or at the top of your closet. Keep the bath towels in the cabinet in your bathroom or on a shelf in your bedroom, where you can easily grab one on your way to the shower.

There are other cute ways to store towels in wine racks and crates; just do a quick Pinterest search to find a thousand ideas. I store my special linens with my fine china, my holiday table linens with my holiday decorations, and my everyday table linens in a kitchen drawer.

Once your linen closet is empty, you've just cleared out prime real estate for storage. My dear friend Leanne Ely, from www.savingdinner.com, likes using the linen closet as a pantry for canned goods and bulky kitchen supplies. Genius! Go ahead and stock up, with the luxury of space you've created.

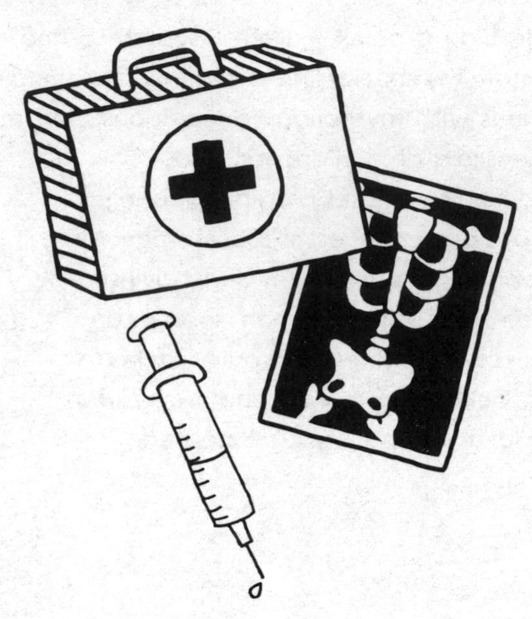

MEDICINE CABINET

Prognosis Is Good

When you are sick, the last thing you want to do is run to the pharmacy. Having a fully stocked medicine cabinet can help smooth out this stressful time.

Set your timer for 10 minutes and get ready to cure the medicine cabinet CHAOS.

1. **Toss out those ancient medications.** Throw away any medications that are past their due date—they aren't effective anymore and may even be harmful. Don't flush these down the toilet. If you live in a city or where there is a community water facility, flushing them down the toilet allows them to remain in the water supply. The best way to dispose of old

medications and pharmaceuticals is to take them to a pharmacy, which has a place to discard them.

2. **Over-the-counter must-haves:** Make a list of the basic medical supplies that you need to have in your medicine cabinet, such as

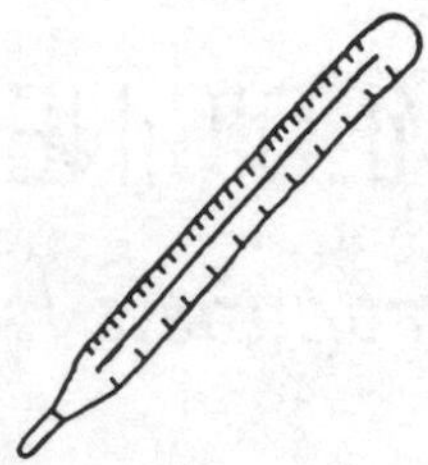

- Pain reliever
- Fever reducer for children if you have little ones
- Antihistamine
- Antibiotic cream
- Antacids
- Saline nose sprays
- Epsom salts
- Nausea medicine, like Pepto-Bismol

You might also like to add

- Adhesive bandages
- Thermometer
- Ace bandage
- Electrolyte solution, such as Pedialyte, made into popsicles (store them in the freezer)
- Nausea medication, such as Emetrol, for children
- Air freshener

Put the items you need on your grocery list or order them online in one batch. Don't spend a fortune—keep it simple! Generic brands do nicely.

Now, let's consider where you're keeping all these medications. Are they in your bathroom? That may not be the best spot because heat, light, and moisture can affect the chemical makeup of the drugs. It's better to store them in a cool, dry place where steam and heat won't reach them. All medications, prescription or otherwise, should be kept away from children at all times.

Clearing out your linen closet (see page 117) will give you a place to keep your medications. If you're on the road a lot, keep a travel bag ready with medical supplies. When you get home from a trip, tuck the bag in your bedroom closet. You'll love having it as a backup.

MAKE YOUR OFFICE WORK FOR YOU

A home office is both a gift and a potential hazard zone. On the one hand, it makes it theoretically possible to put in a full day at work while wearing our jammies. On the other hand, it's a prime Hot Spot for paper clutter to accumulate to avalanche levels. Before long, every surface can get so covered in paper, there's no place left to work. Even the printer gets stacked a mile high with unclaimed printouts.

I can just hear some of you insisting that you're incredibly efficient in that cluttered office and that what looks like CHAOS to the rest of us is really just your system in action.

My experience, however, is that the more cluttered the workspace, the less efficient the results. If your system is working well for you (and anyone else in your family who shares the office), then you can skip this section. But if your "system" makes it tough for you (and them) to find what you need when you need it, I'm talking to you!

The biggest cause of paper clutter, of course, is fear of tossing something out because you might need it one day. Then there's worry about identity theft when you throw away anything printed with personal information. And so, on it goes, and up and up pile the papers.

In the digital age, the rules about what paper to keep, and for how long, have changed. Gone are the days when keeping paper receipts and hard copies of paid bills was the only easy way to track your payments. To avoid identity theft, invest in a good shredder and shred the papers that you no longer need.

On the Fly!

Pace yourself. When organizing paperwork, do not pull everything out at once. Sort one 6-inch stack of papers at a time using the OHIO method: Only Handle It Once.

With that in mind, it's time to tackle that paper, one pint-size pile at a time.

1. Put the papers on your desk into a box. If you have giant piles, divide your desktop into three sections: left, right, and center, and place all the papers in three corresponding boxes. This will help you keep the papers relatively ordered while you prepare them for organizing.

2. Wipe down the desk and leave it bare of everything except the tools you absolutely need (stapler, paper clips, hole punch, etc.). Working with one box at a time, sort the papers into three piles: Toss (flyers and other nonsensitive items that can go right in the recycling), Shred (anything you don't need that includes personal information useful to identity thieves), and Keep.

3. Clear out the Toss and Shred piles. Notice that this room is already looking and feeling a million times better.

4. Further divide your Keep pile into the following subsections: Action Required (such as bills to be paid) and To File (such as receipts, completed tax returns, and other essential documents such as birth or marriage certificates).

5. Create designated homes for each of these two types, such as an inbox for Action Required items and subdivided hanging files for your To File stack.

On the Fly!

Sort all your mail immediately as it comes into your home. See page 129 for more on how to handle mail.

Once your office is in order, make it really great. This is an important part of your home, and a place where you spend a good deal of time. The nicer you make it, the more motivated you'll be to keep it that way. Indulge in quality office supplies, colorful pencils, pens, sticky notes, and a beautiful calendar. Keep your supplies in their proper places in your drawers or other good storage system.

Stick with it!
Where to put it:
In your desk drawer
What to write:
Dead pens = ugly clutter

GET OUT OF MAIL JAIL

Tell me if this sounds familiar: You arrive home with your arms already full, only to be confronted by a mailbox stuffed with bills, newspapers, catalogs, credit card applications, magazines, and packages. You step inside and dump it all on the nearest flat surface, where it joins the bills, newspapers, catalogs, credit card applications, magazines, and packages from the day before. And there it all stays, forming an ever-growing, seemingly insurmountable mountain of doom that you just can't muster the energy to deal with. No wonder you're overwhelmed.

And now we're going to tackle that mountain. But first, let's look a little more closely at why we're having this problem. We're in a big hurry and trying to do too many things at once. We continually tell ourselves that we don't have time, but what we really mean is we don't have time to do it perfectly. That perfectionism is stopping us dead in our tracks and translates to giant piles of procrastination on every open surface.

Whether it's a basket by the door, an entryway console, or the dining table, the place where your mail collects is a prime Hot Spot, and it can make anyone nuts.

On the Fly!

Protect yourself from identity theft by investing in a good shredder. Keep a cardboard box beside it, where you can toss credit card applications, anything with a "preapproval code," or other special offers that include your personal information.

Set your timer for 10 minutes, grab the recycling bin, a trash can, and a shredder, and then sort that toppling stack of mail into the following piles:

RECYCLE
TRASH
PAY
FILE
SHRED

Now that the existing mail is under control, we need a routine with rules for dealing with incoming mail in the future. If you make it a priority, that daily handful of mail will not take long to sort into its proper places.

Most of the mail you receive can go directly into the trash or recycling. Toss out the catalogs, advertisements, notices of special offers, and other junk the instant you walk in the door, before they ever touch a tabletop. Put bills in your Pay pile, important papers in your File pile, and anything with personal information in the box for shredding.

Spend a few minutes processing the paper as soon as you get home, and put everything in its place right away. Your new routine will keep it from piling back up.

On the Fly!

Establish a single spot to store bills that need to be paid.

Got Kids? *Kids love to use the paper shredder. On the next rainy afternoon, point them toward the box and let them have at it!*

Stick with it!
Where to put it:
Where your bills are stored
What to write:
All bills go here

A PLACE OF YOUR OWN

Do you have a place in your home that's important to you and all your own? I hope you do. We all need a place that we can call ours, a place to be creative or think or just rest. Remember how Virginia Woolf said we need "a room of one's own"? That's true, though it doesn't have to be a whole room—it can be a chair in a corner or a space by a window. It doesn't matter where it is, it just has to be *yours*.

This is a place reserved for you to fill with the things that make you smile and lift your heart. Equally important is that it be off limits to the rest of the family unless you've specifically invited them there. A precious child curled on your lap as you read her a story is just the sort of visitor to host there.

I turned our extra bedroom into that kind of room for me. The walls are filled with beautiful photos, artwork, and inspirational verses. My vanity is here, along with my sewing machine. The bay window is decorated with lovely hanging panels of stained glass that catch the afternoon sunbeams. Everything in this room has a special meaning for me, and it makes me happy to be here.

If you already have a place of your own, great! If you don't, I challenge you to create one. Spend 15 minutes turning this space into your haven at home.

You will want to have

- A comfortable chair
- A table with a drawer for personal items
- A lamp to help you see on rainy days
- A blanket to throw over the back of the chair for curling up on cold afternoons
- Your favorite books if you have room for a small bookcase
- A pad of paper and pen for dreaming
- A small bag of items for pampering yourself: hand lotion, nail polish, aromatherapy oil
- A novel, a puzzle book, or a book of daily inspiration
- Photos, plaques, and artwork that touch your heart
- Headphones for your favorite music
- A pretty vase (and treat yourself to flowers regularly)

Use this space to take breaks, relax, and reenergize every day. Whether you live by yourself or with a big family, setting aside a space that's just for joy lets you show up for others—and yourself—in a more meaningful way.

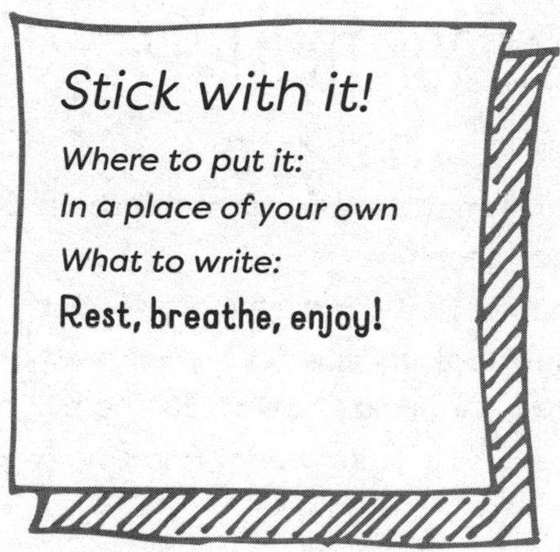

Stick with it!
Where to put it:
In a place of your own
What to write:
Rest, breathe, enjoy!

REFRESH YOUR HOME, REFRESH *YOU* (Plus: Cookies!)

Sometimes our homes just need some fresh air. Open the windows! The doors, too!

If it's too cold for that—and even if it's not—try baking cookies. The smell of baking cookies makes every home happy. When the scent of baking cookies fills the air, you'll feel your mood lift along with it. Here are some recipes you can try.

BASIC COOKIE RECIPE

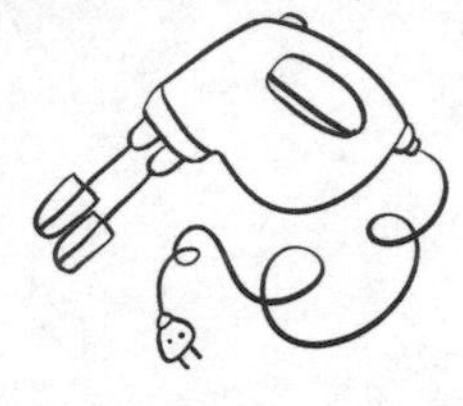

Tools you will need: cookie sheet, parchment paper, hand mixer, plastic wrap, mixing spoon, and cooling rack

After making basic cookie dough, add the variation ingredients, place the dough on plastic wrap, form into a log, and refrigerate for at least 2 hours or overnight (best). You are making your own slice-and-bake cookies.

Cut a 1½-inch slice off the log, then cut it into four pieces like a pie. Roll each piece into a ball with your hands. Place the dough balls on parchment paper 3 inches apart, fill up the cookie sheet (about a dozen), and bake. Put extra dough back in the refrigerator to keep cool.

For cookie bars, all the variations can be pressed into a 13 × 9 pan. Bake at 350 degrees for 30 minutes. Allow cookies to cool completely before cutting. The bars are really easy to remove when you use parchment paper at the bottom of the pan.

I bake all cookies at 350 degrees for 10 to 12 minutes. Adjust cooking time according to how you like cookies. The first batch is always a test batch because we all live at different elevations and ovens cook at different temperatures. Cook longer if you like crispy cookies.

Cream together with hand mixer:

1 cup of softened butter

2 eggs

¾ cup of white granulated sugar

¾ cup of packed brown sugar

1 teaspoon vanilla extract

Slowly stir in:

2¼ cups of self-rising flour

This recipe is a base for almost any cookie you want to bake. If you have the ingredients on hand, you can bake some cookies! Don't be afraid to mess up. The smell of the cookies baking is going to make everyone happy. If something goes wrong, then do like my husband did once: while the cookies were warm he wadded them up in a ball and allowed them to cool. They were still yummy to me. You can double the recipe and freeze the dough for later or for emergencies.

VARIATIONS

CHOCOLATE CHIP COOKIES

2 cups of chocolate chips

1 cup of chopped nuts (optional)

M&M COOKIES

2 cups of M&Ms

OATMEAL COOKIES

3 cups of rolled oats

1 tsp of cinnamon

PLAIN SUGAR COOKIES

Omit the brown sugar

Double the amount of white granulated sugar

Reduce to 1 egg

Increase self-rising flour by ½ cup

Roll in colored sugar before baking or decorate with icing after baking

PEANUT BUTTER COOKIES

Increase white and brown sugar by ¼ cup each

Add 1 cup of creamy peanut butter

Increase flour by ¼ cup

Gently smash the rolled dough balls with a damp fork to make crosshatches

PECAN SANDIES

2 cups of chopped pecans

CHOCOLATE COOKIES

¾ cup of cocoa

3 tbsp of powdered sugar

Roll dough balls in powdered sugar and bake

SNICKERDOODLES

Add 2 tsp cream of tartar

Increase flour by ½ cup

Mix 1 tsp of cinnamon with 2 tbsp of granulated sugar

Roll dough balls in the cinnamon-sugar mixture and bake

BROWNIES

Add ¾ cup of cocoa

Omit brown sugar and add an extra ½ cup of white sugar

Reduce butter by ¼ cup and melt

Add 2 extra eggs

Reduce flour by 1 cup

Add 1 cup of chocolate chips

Add 1 cup of chopped nuts (optional)

Pour batter into greased or parchment paper–lined 13 × 9 pan and bake for 30 minutes

Allow to cool completely before cutting

On the Fly!

Parchment paper makes your life easier. No mess and no messing up cookies trying to get them off the cookie sheet. Just slide the paper right onto the cooling rack.

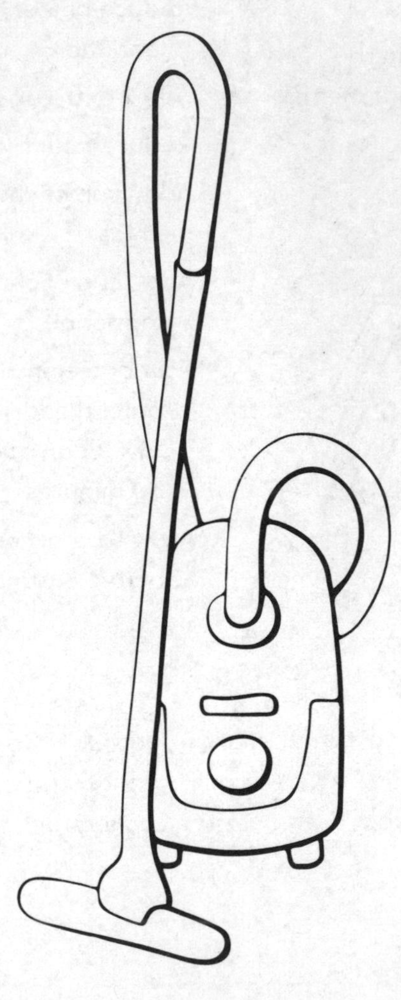

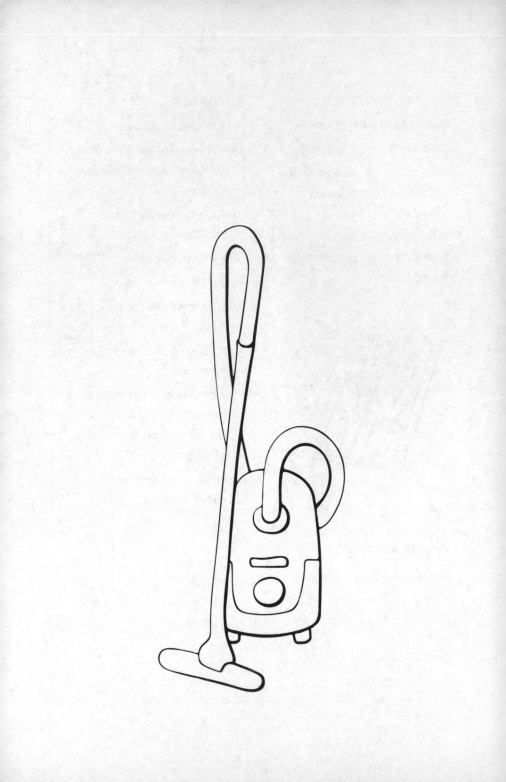

JUST THE MIDDLES

Quick Attacks for Your Floors

Pick a room, people. It's time to vacuum. If you've got hardwood floors, you can substitute a broom—either way, it's time to get the grime gone. Set your timer for 5 minutes.

First, find the floor. I mean it! If there's anything underfoot that's not supposed to be there—anything that's not furniture or otherwise a permanent fixture in the room—do the Hot Spot Shuffle and set it aside. We're staying focused on vacuuming and we will not be sidetracked by decluttering.

Get your vacuum and get going. You know what to do. Most days you only need to do a quickie clean—just do the middles and don't move the furniture. When you're finished, check your timer and see how long it actually took you. I'll bet you still have time left over.

On the Fly!

Don't make it hard on yourself. Even just doing the middles is better than procrastinating. A clean floor makes every room feel fresh and new, and you'll sense the difference right away.

Got Kids? *Make memories and get your floors mopped at the same time. Put the kids in their bathing suits, spray some shaving cream on the floor with a little water, and let them slip and slide with some old damp towels. You'll have the kids and their friends begging to mop! Just make sure to rinse and dry their feet before they leave the kitchen so that they don't tromp shaving cream through the house.*

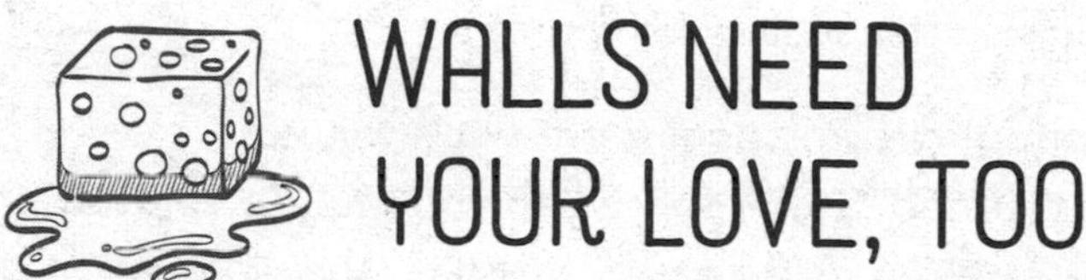

WALLS NEED YOUR LOVE, TOO

Yep. Even the walls need to be washed once in a while. Here are some of the reasons why:

→ There are certain spots that we and our families touch pretty much every day without even noticing it—over the stair banister, next to light switches, around doorknobs. Over time, these spots get grimy and germy.

→ Grease not only splatters around the stove but also can build up on the walls. (If you fry a lot of food, this one's for you!)

→ Using your fireplace, or even burning a lot of candles, causes soot to build up on the walls.

→ If you smoke (or if you move into a place last inhabited by a smoker), the paint can get discolored.

→ Hairspray leaves a grimy buildup on bathroom walls.

→ Two-year-olds think that a blank wall and a box of crayons spell an invitation to create.

→ If you want to paint, the walls will need a good once-over first in order for the paint to adhere properly. (I've learned the hard way that if you skip this step, you'll regret it!)

Under normal circumstances, our walls will not need to be cleaned often—only when you make a splatter or your child uses them as a canvas. Washing the walls is just a simple matter of wiping down the surfaces with a wet cloth. It takes only a few seconds to clean those grimy areas. Don't make a huge deal out of it!

Visit **flylady.net** to find two great tools to help with wall washing: microfiber cloths (silver rags) and a Rubba Scrubba (this puppy can even erase crayon marks!). You can attach a microfiber cloth to a FlyLady mop to avoid climbing a ladder while washing walls.

When you're cleaning, wipe down the light switches and doorknobs, too—this helps keep germs at bay.

On the Fly!

Trim wicks on candles to keep the smoke down and avoid gray streaks forming on your walls. If you're really struggling with this, try electric candles. No soot!

THE WRITING ON THE WALL

Chalk It Up to Organization

We love seeing chalkboard walls in coffee shops and trendy restaurants, but did you know you could have chalkboard walls in your own home, too? Painting one wall in your kitchen with chalkboard paint could be functional as well as a focal point.

Let's think about this for a minute. Where can you use a little chalkboard paint?

- → Kitchen walls
- → Refrigerator doors
- → Child's bedroom
- → Office walls
- → Canisters in your pantry
- → Dresser drawers

On the Fly!

Take a picture of your wall with the grocery list on it before you leave home each day. This way, if you get a chance to run by the market, you can pick up items on your list.

Painting a wall with chalkboard paint gives you an always-handy spot to jot notes, leave messages, and post reminders. If you have an artistic hand, you can get creative and colorful while you're doing it.

Here are a few clever ways you can use a chalkboard wall to your advantage:

→ Keep current with your grocery list.

→ Plan menus for the week.

→ Leave notes for family members or roommates.

→ Remind yourself of important to-dos.

→ Keep children occupied while you're cooking.

→ Enjoy the inspiration of famous quotes and important sayings.

→ Label drawers with the contents.

Chalkboard paint comes in a tub and in a spray can, and whichever way you like to paint, the effect is both snazzy *and* smart. Choose a wall that's easily reachable and give it a good coating—better yet, two or three! Be sure the paint is completely dry before marking it with chalk.

A chalkboard wall is a great place to put information you

refer to frequently, such as a morning routine or a weekly schedule. Meanwhile, there's no need to limit your chalkboard strategy to the wall—why not paint your refrigerator or a tabletop? This can give a new look to your kitchen.

Your office is also a great place for a chalkboard wall. You can write down your goals and inspirational quotes of your mentors, and maybe get creative by painting a huge calendar on the wall in front of your face.

If you live in a home where painting walls isn't permitted, chalkboarding is still an option for you. You can buy rolls of contact paper to turn into chalkboards that you can remove from the walls later. There are also chalkboard stickers, labels, and decals available in a range of sizes and shapes. Pair them with a set of chalkboard pens in a few colors and you're ready to go.

Here is one little warning: Don't overwhelm yourself. If you jump in to paint a wall, a room, or your refrigerator without already having your home in order, you are going to be adding to the mess.

On the Fly!

Warning: Reminders on walls tend to get ignored because they blend in with the décor. If you have an important reminder, don't leave it to the wall to remind you—take a picture of it and text it to yourself.

HUNG UP ON HANGING ART

Perfectionism just loves to crop up when we start thinking about decorating the walls. Pinterest is full of wildly intimidating gallery walls that look like they were assembled by a fleet of design professionals. And, of course, that's because they were. For us mere mortals just trying to make our houses feel like home, all those images are the stuff of months—sometimes years—of procrastination.

What if I hang it all in the wrong configuration? Should all the frames match? Is it okay to mix artwork with photos? We're so afraid of making a mistake that the walls stay bare.

The only actual rule of creating a wall display is that *you* love the way it looks, so stop worrying and get hanging. We no longer live in a time when a nail hole can ruin a wall. Products like 3M Command Hooks and Picture Hanging Strips eliminate the need for a hammer and nails anyway. The beauty of these handy devices is that if we make a mistake, we can easily fix it without ruining the paint. I keep a drawer full of assorted sizes and shapes for any sort of hanging project. (You will, of course, still have to find a stud and use a nail occasionally if you are hanging a large mirror or a heavier piece of artwork.)

MAKE A DISPLAY

I love the homey, eclectic look of mismatched frames, photos, and artwork that have nothing in common other than the fact that they look interesting together. Feel free to hang framed kids' artwork side by side with formal paintings, wedding photos with silly snapshots, an inspirational quote next to a framed scrap of baby blanket.

If you crave more structure, it can be helpful to find a unifying theme that ties things together. For example, the frames can all be the same color or material, the photos can all be black-and-white or color, or each piece can represent a special family memory in some way. If you'd like more help, do an internet search for free downloadable wall templates, complete with exact frame measurements and spacing recommendations. You can then print the template you like best and order frames for that layout.

For even more structure, do an internet search for "gallery in a box" and you'll find all sorts of prepackaged sets that include not only all the frames but also the exact configuration in which they should be hung. Then all you have to add are your own photos and artwork.

DON'T BURY YOUR BEAUTIES

Most of us store the vast majority of our photos in our phones or in the cloud, where they'll theoretically last forever. In reality, though, they're enjoyed only by our Facebook friends and Instagram followers on the day we post them and after that by no one at all. Get those great memories out of the cloud and onto your walls where you and your family can enjoy them every day. Do an internet search for "online photo printing" to find countless sites that will send you beautiful, affordable prints of your uploaded photos to frame.

OFF THE WALL: DIGITAL OPTIONS

It's wonderful to have walls that honor you with photos of happy times or that delight you with color and pattern. But having uncluttered walls can be refreshing, too. I like to enjoy some of my own photos *off* the walls: My TV has a screensaver that displays digital photographs, and so does my computer. You can also get digital picture frames that hold and display hundreds of photos in a continuous slideshow.

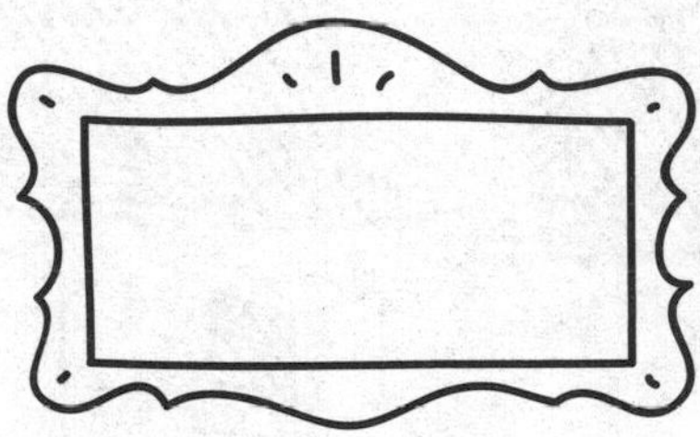

GARAGE SNEAK ATTACK
(Works for Basements, Too!)

When you open your garage door, does the cumulative real estate value of your neighborhood drop significantly? Have you piled things so high that you can no longer open the door? Does your new car sit out in the weather because there's no room to park her inside?

Don't beat yourself up over this. We've all been there!

The Sneak Attack is an approach that works for the garage, the basement, that extra junk room, or any other space you find too intimidating to inhabit for any length of time. It has taken years for this garage to get in this shape, and there is no way that you can get it all cleaned out in a day. That's fine! **Progress not perfection!** The most important thing is to stop ignoring the problem by giving it small bursts of attention, bit by bit.

Here's what you're going to do. Set your timer for minutes. That's right, just 5 minutes. This room is too overwhelming for anything longer.

Once your timer is set, open the door to the garage (or basement). Poke your head in, grab the box closest to the door, and run to a pleasant spot in your home, having closed the door behind you.

Safely settled in a happy spot, open the box. Toss out the trash, put away usable items, and gather any items to give away. Those go straight to your car.

And that's it.

This is how it's going to get clean. Just do 5 minutes each day. At first it won't seem like you're even making a dent, but don't quit before the miracle happens. If you're discouraged, celebrate the fact that you're actually doing something instead of ignoring the demons in the dungeon. And when you start to see open floor space and uncluttered shelves, you'll enjoy the feeling of calm confidence that you deserve.

I am so proud of you for tackling this forgotten room.

Stick with it!
Where to put it:
By the garage door
What to write:
Toss two items

LET'S GET A MOVE ON

Sports and Camping Gear

Having an active lifestyle adds a whole new dimension to our home organization and routines. Where do we put all that gear and stuff? Every sport has its paraphernalia! And when you love that sport, you are going to collect more stuff to go along with it. The big question is: Where should you put it?

I have a few rules:

1. If it stinks or needs to dry, it goes in the garage or basement.
2. If critters might make a home in it, it needs to live inside.
3. If it needs washing, it goes immediately into the washer.

These rules help me to be prepared for my next outing.

Nothing puts a damper on getting a move on like having to gather up stuff before I can leave. Try these best practices and you'll get your gear in gear.

On the Fly!

Make a permanent Camping and Vacation Packing list and keep it in your phone or on your computer.

WORKOUT CLOTHES

The laundry room is where these items are placed as part of your afternoon routine when you get home. This way, no bad smells will come from the bedrooms.

1. Each day this gear needs to be laundered to keep it from stinking up the house.
2. Then repack it in the duffle bag, ready for tomorrow and placed on your Launch Pad.
3. Or place this clean clothing in the bathroom, ready for you to put on the next morning.

The longer these items of clothing sit in a hamper, the more they will stink. This is the Do It Now principle at its best. It stops the smell from getting worse.

Sport shoes are another issue altogether. The reason they smell so bad is because they are never allowed to air out and dry. A little sunshine can be good for them, too. I have even been known to put my shoes over a vent to completely dry them out. Having two pairs of shoes that you rotate can help with the smell.

Once everything is clean and dry, it can be packed into a duffle bag, ready to go. No more searching for everything you need for your activity.

SPORTS EQUIPMENT

The more you have, the more you need a dedicated space to store it. If you have a garage or basement, that's an ideal spot that will allow it to air out between uses. Hooks and shelving can accommodate most items. Large items, such as canoes and kayaks, may need to be stored outside. They can be suspended under decks—just be sure you turn them upside down to prevent water from filling them.

On the Fly!

Keep a kitchen bin for outdoor-kitchen cooking. Include paper plates, towels, cups, spices, utensils, cookware, camp stove, and a cast-iron Dutch oven for making dessert. See page 159 for my yummy Dutch Oven Peach Cobbler recipe.

CAMPING GEAR

Camping is a fun way to spend a weekend. Just don't make it such an ordeal that you dread going. You can make lots of fun memories, but only if you ditch your angst about not having every little helpful item with you.

Make it easy on yourself by using decluttered Rubbermaid

bins for your camping supplies: cooking bin, sleeping bin, hygiene bin. I like to list all the items in each bin. These lists are put into a sheet protector and taped to the lids with heavy-duty packing tape. I also keep this list in my phone. Then the only thing you need to do to leave is grab your bins, ice chest, and tents and stop by the grocery to get food for the camping trip. I even keep a list of food for the adventure. A few minutes of planning makes for an amazing weekend around a campfire.

It is a good idea to keep a supply of s'mores ingredients and roasting sticks stashed away, not only for camping but for those spur-of-the-moment evening fires. Always be sure to check the local fire danger level with the fire department or forest service.

The secret to making camping easy on yourself is to replenish what you use, dry the tents if they are damp, and air out the sleeping bags as soon as you get home, while it is fresh in your mind. Then repack everything to get ready for your next adventure. You'll be good to go!

This whole system also works for long vacations or a day at the beach.

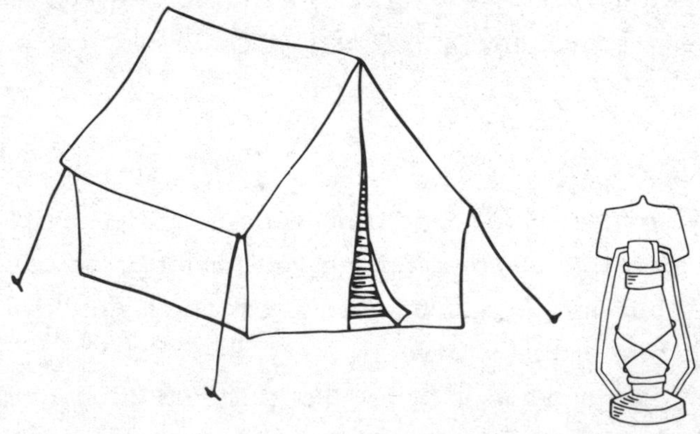

DUTCH OVEN PEACH COBBLER

2 30-ounce cans of sliced peaches in syrup

1 box of yellow cake mix

½ stick of butter cut into pieces

Cinnamon and sugar

Pour peaches into the Dutch oven, sprinkle the dry cake mix over the peaches, add slices of butter on top, and sprinkle with cinnamon and sugar. Put the lid on and place 10 hot coals on the lid for even cooking.

Place the Dutch oven close to the fire for 45 minutes or until done. Serve with ice cream or whipped cream.

On the Fly!

Cleanup is a breeze with cast-iron Dutch oven liners.

A HOT MESS ON WHEELS

Car Care Is Self-Care

Car clutter gets in the way of being kind to others.

There was a time when I practically lived out of my car. This would have been fine had it not been for a sea of fast-food wrappers and empty drink cups from the dollar menu at the drive-through, which perfectly suited my budget. Looking back, I can't figure out why I didn't just toss out past wrappers when I was waiting in line for my next meal. Instead, I told myself that I'd clear out the trash at home, and then I never would. I lived in a constant state of car shame.

Not only is it unpleasant to drive in a cluttered car, but it gets in the way of being helpful to others. I dodged requests for rides whenever I could.

Eventually, I got rid of that car and traded it in for a shiny pickup truck, and I established a set of rules for myself to keep it clean.

My new rules of the road were:

1. No more eating in the car. If I needed food while I was out, I had to go into a restaurant. This kept my car clean and helped me to think more carefully about the food I was eating.

2. Take out what you put in. Anything I brought into the car in the morning had to come out of it at the end of the day.

3. When I filled up the tank with gas, I took the opportunity to put trash in the bin.

That's it. Easy, doable. And it made a big difference. If you follow these rules, it will take less than 5 minutes a day and your car will be a much calmer space.

I no longer live out of my vehicle, I'm happy to say. But that doesn't mean I don't need to maintain my car with care. I am always prepared if there is an emergency. Here is my list of items that live in my car:

- Fire extinguisher
- Flashlight
- Extra money
- Orange reflective vest
- Can of Fix-a-Flat or air pump
- Duct tape
- A regular blanket and fold-up Mylar emergency blanket
- Rubber gloves and work gloves

- → First aid kit
- → Umbrella
- → Change of clothes
- → Hat
- → Rain jacket
- → Small tool kit
- → Car emergency kit (jumper cables, reflectors)
- → Your car's owner's manual
- → Simple survival kit: water, energy bars, small fold-up shovel
- → Trash bag
- → Window cleaner and a FlyLady Purple Rag for washing the windshield
- → FlyLady Rubba Sweepa for clearing snow from the car
- → Tissues
- → Paper towels

You may not need all these items—choose what's right for your car and your life. But, for me, I like knowing I have every item on this list. Just like in my home, everything has a place and everything is in its place. Some of it's in the trunk, and some is in a bin underneath my backseat. Use the trunk of your car or the back area, but the items need to be contained or strapped down.

I've thought about eliminating a few items, but I never know when I might need to help someone or myself. I could be stranded on the highway in a snowstorm and need a blanket while I wait for roadside service, or my sunroof could break and I'd be thankful that I had duct tape to keep the rain out. I once had to change a tire on a country road, and I was grateful I had the proper clothes and protective equipment I needed.

Our cars get so messy because we are often in a hurry when we are using them, and when we are in a hurry, our attention to our surroundings goes out the window. Let's slow down and take time to enjoy the journey! Build in grace time to get where you're going, resist the urge to rush, and practice patience as you drive. We'll all be cleaner, calmer, and kinder—not to mention safer—if we do.

On the Fly!

If you don't have an owner's manual, you can usually find a PDF online for your make and model. Print it out and put it in your car—you never know when you might need it.

MAINTENANCE

Funnily enough, cars need to be maintained. The oil needs changing, the tires need rotating, and windshield wipers need replacing. I know you know this, but do you do this?

Are you up to speed with your car care? When the little light comes on to remind you to take it in for maintenance, don't ignore it. That light gives you plenty of time to make that appointment, but when you procrastinate, you create chaos for yourself because one day your car will refuse to take you where you want to go.

Have you ever read your owner's manual? Make it a point to read it from start to finish. Once upon a time, I had a little sports car whose windshield wipers turned on all by themselves. Who knew they made windshield wipers that detected raindrops? I thought there was a malfunction! The owner's manual explained it all.

Good habits with your car care will save you loads of trouble and money. Don't skimp, and don't procrastinate.

Stick with it!
Where to put it:
On your dashboard
What to write:
What goes in must
come out

PEST PATROL

Roaches, Ants, Spiders, and Other Uninvited Guests

I will never forget moving into our first new home when I was a young mother, only to find ourselves overrun by roaches within months. I had kept the house clean, and just couldn't understand how this had happened. Eventually, I realized that it had nothing to do with the cleanliness of our home.

At one time or another in the years since, we've had moths, weevils, spiders, ants, gnats, fleas, and mice. The one good thing about this is that I've learned all the tricks in the book for getting rid of them and keeping them out, and now I can share them with you.

My best advice is to clean up after yourself and avoid leaving food exposed. Simple habits strung into routines go a long way to keeping unwanted critters out of your home. If they still get in despite your best efforts, just don't beat yourself up over it. It happens to the best of us.

ROACHES

These nasty critters are hitchhikers and find all sorts of creative ways to get in, from bags of potatoes to paper sacks to empty cardboard boxes. The most important trick to keeping them at bay is to limit their food source. That means: Throw food scraps away immediately instead of leaving them on the counter. You can also

→ Seal food in containers.

→ Remove potatoes from bags and put them into a bowl.

→ Take out the trash daily.

→ Put paper sacks and shipping boxes directly outside into the recycling.

→ Repair any water leaks (roaches need water).

If the roaches have already taken hold, use a product with boric acid to kill them. And if you still need help, bring on the exterminator.

MOTHS AND WEEVILS

These pests sneak in via the food we bring home. Once, we got them in a box of unopened oatmeal. The little larvae ate their way out of a cardboard box, started flying around everywhere, got into closets, and destroyed beloved sweaters. They were driving us nuts, so we searched everywhere for the source. It wasn't until I went to the pantry to make breakfast that I discovered the box where it had all started, and let's just say

it was several months before I could look at a bowl of oatmeal again.

How do we deal with this when it comes in from the grocery store?

When you bring home a bag of flour, store it in the freezer for a month at 0 degrees.

Decant your flour and oats into clear, sealable canisters.

Try not to stress if you suspect that your food has been contaminated. When in doubt, just throw it out and let it go.

Stick with it!
Where to put it:
By the trash
What to write:
Don't get bugged.
Take out the trash.

SPIDERS

I have a love/hate relationship with spiders. As a child, I loved *Charlotte's Web*. Spiders also eat those mosquitoes, wasps, and flying beetles that prey on us. I like spiders when they're outside, but I don't like to be surprised by them in the house.

Spiders, as we know, like to hide. Our mission, then, is to eliminate their hideouts whenever we can.

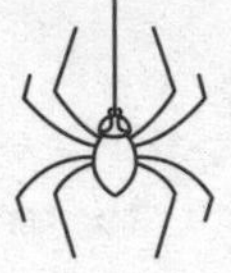

- Once a month take a feather duster or broom to all the rooms in your home to wipe out cobwebs. Also dust behind your headboard and under your bed.
- Clean out toy boxes and other clutter sites.
- Never leave shoes outside.
- Store shoes that you rarely wear in clear plastic shoeboxes.
- If you see a spider, catch it with a glass, slide cardboard under the glass, and put it outside.

You may not like spiders, but they do good work. Except for the poisonous ones, of course, like the black widow and brown recluse. Look them up so you can recognize them (and avoid panicking when you come across one of their harmless cousins!).

GNATS

When fruit is in season, we love having a bowl readily available for our family. When you store fruit in the refrigerator, no one eats it; out of sight, out of mind. But with fruit out on the counter, before you know it, those fruit flies start popping up everywhere and multiplying like crazy.

How do we deal with them?

- Wash your fruit when you bring it home.
- Store the fruit in the refrigerator and pull out just a few pieces at a time.
- When the gnats gather, catch them with a trap: Place some fruit, fruit juice, apple cider vinegar, or wine in the bottom of a small glass. Add a couple of drops of dishwashing liquid. The gnats will drown themselves.

→ You can also put a little vinegar in a glass and cover it with plastic wrap, then poke small holes in the plastic wrap so the gnats can get in but they can't get out.

→ Don't leave dirty dishes on kitchen counters.

ANTS

Every spring brings the Great Ant Invasion. I hate them. If you see one ant, then watch out—if it heads back home with food for the colony, it'll soon return with the whole clan.

There are three types of ants: grease ants, sugar ants, and carpenter ants. The first two are tiny. The carpenter ants are large and have wings that drop off and leave an even more unpleasant deposit. In the South, there are also fire ants that bite. If you have those, get an exterminator right away. They can hurt you and your children if they are disturbed.

How to get rid of ants in your home:

→ Keep all ant-killing products out of the reach of children and pets.

→ Put your sugar in a sealed container, not just a sugar bowl.

→ In a jar lid, mix together 1 teaspoon of powdered sugar and 2 teaspoons of boric acid. Place in the path of the ants.

→ Every winter, place an order online for ant bait or boric acid so you'll have it locked and loaded when spring rolls around. You'll have these products when you need to kill them. If you wait to purchase them until the time you need these supplies, everyone else needs them then, too, and supplies could run low. Put this on your calendar to remind you to place the order in February.

→ Look for openings around drain lines and water lines. You may need to caulk these areas.

→ Even if you do everything right, often ants still invade. Put out the bait and you'll keep them at bay for another year.

FLEAS

One spring we rescued a dog we named Chief. The only carpet in our home is in the office, and that dog loved to follow my husband down there. Before we knew it, the office was infested with fleas. We tried everything to get rid of them. The bottom line is that if you have pets, the fleas will hitch a ride inside with them.

The key to keeping your place from getting infested (and keeping your pets happy) is to take decisive action at the very first sign of these little sneaks. Bathe your pets with a flea shampoo, and treat them monthly with oral or topical flea prevention treatments (ask the salesperson at the pet supply store which product works best for the type of fleas in your area).

Also, you can buy some diatomaceous earth (available online or at pet supply stores), sprinkle it on the carpet, and let it sit for a day before vacuuming it up. Diatomaceous earth is not poisonous to pets, so it is even okay to sprinkle it directly on their fur if you choose.

MICE

Of all the pests that can invade our homes, mice are about the worst for me. They build nests for their babies out of paper, fabrics, and other items they scrounge from around the house. I once lost a cherished piece of my son's artwork to a mouse, and thinking about it still makes me sad. Sentiment aside, however, I think we can all agree that mouse poop is an unpleasant accent in a home.

Mice find our homes especially tantalizing when the temperature starts to drop. Here's how to stop them coming in:

→ Look for any small openings into your home, whether around pipes, through small holes in walls, or other tiny potential entrances. Stuff these cracks and crevices with bits of steel wool until they're tightly packed enough to prevent a mouse from squeezing through.

→ Set humane traps that capture mice for you to release outdoors or that at least kill them quickly (avoid glue traps because those cause needless suffering). Instead of using cheese as bait for your traps, try a caramel or a dab of peanut butter.

→ If you find a mouse nest, get on your long sleeves, a face mask, and rubber gloves to clean it out. (I found one tucked among our Christmas decorations in the garage one year. The scene was neither merry nor bright.)

→ Store items you love in areas where mice cannot go. They can chew through plastic bins.

→ When all else fails, it never hurts to have a good cat. They make great pets and they love to bring you presents. Life in the jungle.

CRITTERLOVE

Cleaning and Caring for Our Pets

Our pets play a central role in our lives and are as much a part of our families as any of us humans. Our critters are as fond of routines as we are, and they always know when it's time for the next activity. Put on your shoes in the morning, and watch them do a happy dance because they know it's time to go for a walk.

Pets can add a little work to our day, but it's 100 percent worth it for the unconditional love they give us in return. They alert us to dangers and help us relax. Just put a sleepy puppy in your lap and feel how calm you get. Pets are also exceptional judges of character. If my blue tick hound Lucy had not liked Robert on our first date, I doubt he'd have made it to the second round.

Here are some ways that our beloved critters add to our daily, weekly, monthly, and yearly routines.

DAILY

→ Wherever possible, piggyback your pet-related tasks with other things that you already do every day.

→ While your coffee is brewing or you're waiting for your toast, take a minute to dust mop your floors to get up pet hair.

→ When you fill up your water bottle, fill up your pet's water dish, too.

→ Put out food for your pet when you start your own breakfast.

→ If you have a puppy, check for little piddles and poops when you first enter a room.

→ When you go for a walk, take your pet.

→ Before you head to bed, check for items that might be especially tempting to curious critters.

→ Put away pet toys so you don't trip over them during the night on the way to the bathroom.

→ Scoop out the litter box each night before you go to bed.

On the Fly!

Our pets thrive on routines, just like we do. Put your pets on a schedule and they'll reward you with good behavior.

WEEKLY

→ When you make your grocery list, check to see whether your pet's food is running low.

→ Pick a day each week to set aside 30 minutes to relax with and brush your pet.

→ Wash your pet's bowls and clean the area where they are kept.

→ Use a Rubba Scrubba or tape roller to remove pet hair from upholstered furniture.

→ Change the litter in the litter box.

MONTHLY

→ Wash your pet's beds to keep them fresh.

→ Bathe your pet if needed.

→ Trim your pet's nails whenever you schedule your own haircut.

YEARLY

→ When you make an appointment for your own annual physical, make one for your pet's checkup and shots. Put it on your calendar.

→ Order flea and tick collars or topical products in the early spring.

→ Get your pet groomed.

Your pets are part of your family and home. When you take care of them, they'll reward you with love, attention, good health, and good behavior. Enjoy your time with them, and when one of them leaves this world, don't be afraid to love again!

Stick with it!
Where to put it:
By the toaster or coffeepot
What to write:
Sweep the floor and swipe the counter

FIRED UP ABOUT FIREPLACES

I live in the mountains of North Carolina in the middle of 10 acres of hardwood trees. My husband carefully selects trees from our forest to harvest for firewood. If we have a storm and trees fall, they are quickly cut and split to cure for the future. Once, we had a beautiful 60-year-old white oak in our front yard just fall over into our driveway for absolutely no discernible reason. That tree supplied several seasons of firewood for all the people who came to help us remove it. We were very thankful that no one was hurt when that tree sacrificed itself.

In recent years there's been increased awareness of the impact of wood burning on air quality, and we all need to respect our role as stewards of the environment. Be careful to use only the resources you need, and make the most of your fires when you do build them. Our fires not only provide warmth and light but also can be used to cook our food with a cast-iron skillet and to eliminate paper clutter while we're at it. They're also a useful tool for surviving storms when there are power outages. Fireplaces are messy, but they're worth the trouble if you love yours as much as we love ours. Some of my favorite family memories are of days and nights gathered together around a fire.

Living in a forest, I am very aware of fire danger during the dry times of the year. Many forest fires are caused by the ashes from a fireplace. Ashes can hold embers for several days. I knew someone who cleaned out her fireplace, placed the ashes in a cardboard box, and put the box out on the back deck. It wasn't long before the box was ablaze and the deck rail was burning. She got the fire out, but it was a scary lesson learned. Our rule is that when we remove ashes from the fireplace, they go straight into a sealed metal bucket to be left for a week before they're dumped safely in a hole in the woods.

FLYLADY'S MOUNTAIN METHOD OF FIRE BUILDING

We have a cute little saying in our mountains for how to build a fire: One Can't, Two Won't, Three Will! It is a great way to remember the basics of assembling a fire that will stay lit.

You will need:

→ Fireplace tools: poker, shovel, tongs, broom

→ Fire screen

→ A sealed metal bucket for ashes

→ Seasoned firewood

→ Kindling

→ Newspaper (or better yet, paper clutter from your shredding pile)

→ Matches

Here is what you will do:

1. Before you build a fire, make sure that the damper is open. You won't like your home filling up with smoke.

2. Start with some wadded-up pieces of paper.

3. Add three or four fat little pieces of wood (pine kindling).

4. Stack two pieces of firewood on the paper and kindling, and a third piece across the top of those.

5. Light the paper on fire. As the fire strengthens, you can add more wood.

On the Fly!

Make a paste out of ashes and water and use it to polish your silver jewelry.

Enable inside fires to fade by spreading out the logs. Never go to bed or leave a room with a big roaring fire going. Once you're done with a fire outside, extinguish it properly by separating the wood from other pieces and pouring water on the coals. Stir the coals and add more water.

When the fireplace ashes build up, use the shovel to scoop the ashes into the sealed metal bucket. Allow your fireplace ashes to cool for several days. A quick feather dust of the mantle and hearthstone will get rid of the dust and debris. Then restock your indoor wood supply so it's ready for your next fire.

On the Fly!

Ashes have plenty of uses in your garden and yard, and with your pets. They can enhance your compost, prevent garden pests, and de-skunk your dog.

FIREPLACE SAFETY RULES

Above all, keep it safe!

1. Before using a fireplace, double-check that you have a working smoke detector in your home.

2. Make sure the damper is fully open.

3. The wood needs to be dry. Unseasoned wood will deposit creosote in your chimney, which can lead to a chimney fire and extensive smoke damage to your home.

4. Build your fire so that air flows properly and the wood has a chance to burn.

5. Add more wood to build a nice, hot fire to keep the chimney clean.

6. Replace the fire screen to catch any sparks that may pop out of the fire.

7. Keep a fireproof rug in front of your fireplace.

8. Have a little spray bottle of water handy for any sparks that manage to make their way past your fireplace screen.

9. **Never** leave a fire unattended.

10. Keep a fire extinguisher on that floor of your home and know how to use it.

11. Stay aware of the fire danger in your area, and don't build a fire if the danger is high.

12. At least once a week, clean out the ashes and allow them to completely cool for a week before disposing of them.

Stick with it!
Where to put it:
By the fireplace
What to write:
Save the ashes

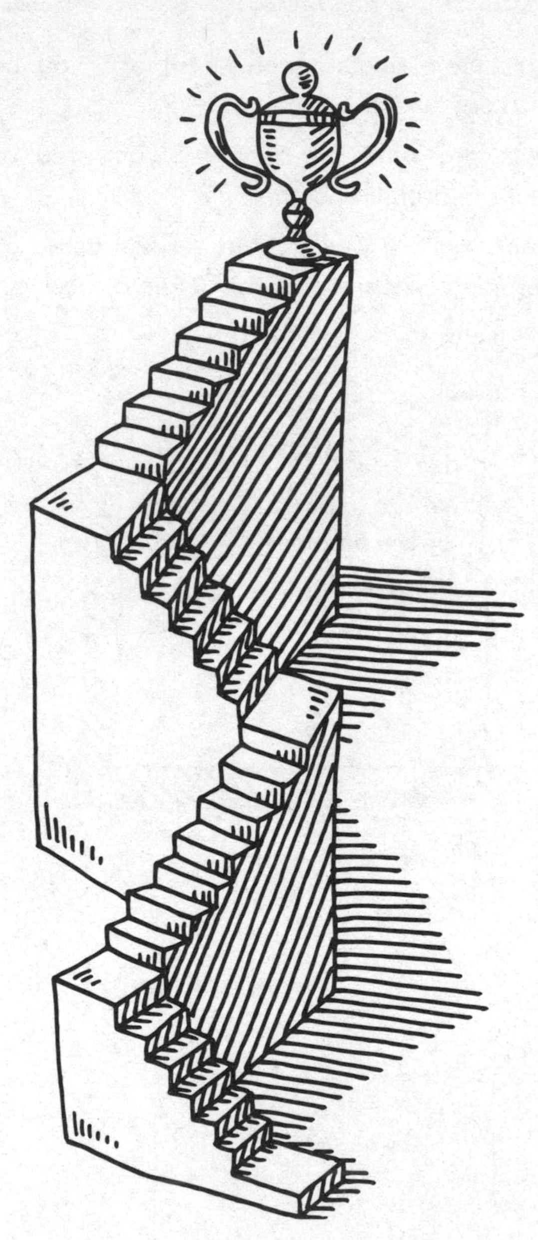

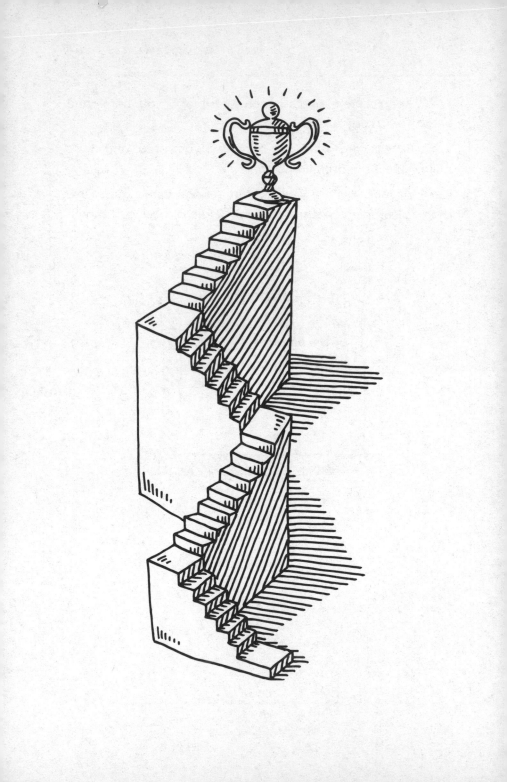

CONCLUSION

DITCH THE DRUDGERY. EMBRACE THE DREAM

Dear Friends,

Whether we know it or not, we are homemakers. We are the creators of our environments. We dream of having a home that is beautiful and efficient, with a place for everything—and with a new attitude embracing us, we can create the homes of our dreams.

All our lives we have looked at caring for our homes as house *work*, a four-letter, ugly word. We have rebelled against it, we have been punished with it, and we have used the chores to punish our own children. We all deserve to live in a home that surrounds us—hugs us—with love.

I hope this book has helped you readjust your attitude from

"housework is drudgery" to "housework honors me and makes my house a loving home." It is an act of self-kindness. Our homes are our sanctuary from a hectic world.

I grew up with Saturday cleaning marathons and an unhappy mother who hated cleaning. We have to get rid of the hatred of the action and recognize that our home needs to be loved. By releasing our perfectionism, we can begin to embrace our homes with the love we have for ourselves and our family.

The perfectionism that was instilled in us from an early age is what causes us to procrastinate. We were taught that if you can't do it right, don't do it at all. This is the one cliché that has stuck with us. We were made to reclean our rooms because they were not done to perfect standards. Now we tell ourselves every day that we don't have time. The funny part is the rest of that sentence is left unsaid: We don't have time *to do it right*. So we put it off, looking for large sections of time to marathon-clean. All of us lead busy lives.

Now you are armed with skills, routines, methods, and, above all, a new attitude that hugs you. These tools will allow you to create the home you have always dreamed of having. I know you can do this, one step at a time.

I love you all!

Love,

The FlyLady

ACKNOWLEDGMENTS

I would like to thank my sister, Patricia Newlin; she has always pushed me out of my comfort zone to write books. Our teamwork since we were children helped us to survive, thrive, and now help others.

To my son, Justin Cain, who gave up his dream to help me to be FlyLady. Thank you for all you do to empower me!

To my Sweet Darlin' husband Robert Cilley! His patience, love, laughter, knowledge, and morning coffee fuels me day in and day out! Sweet Darlins Forever! Poo!

To my FLY Team; Jack, Kathy, Laura, Liz, Michael, and Rebecca. Thank you for all you do to make our FlyBabies' lives easier! We are a team and your love for our FlyBabies shines through everything you do!

To my editor, Laura Mazer. It was a joy to work with you! It did not feel like work at all. I knew the first time we talked on the phone that you could bring out the best in me and I would be willing to let go and allow you to guide me!

ABOUT THE AUTHOR

Marla Cilley, known to her millions of fans and followers as The FlyLady, is an organizing and time management expert with a system she shares with her followers on the website FlyLady.net. She is the author of three previous best-selling books, *Sink Reflections, Body Clutter,* and *CHAOS to Clean*. She lives in the mountains of North Carolina with her Sweet Darlin' Robert and their critters.